FRANK LLOYD WRIGHT

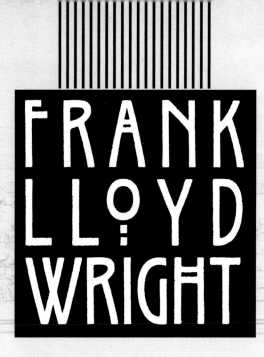

FRANK LLOYD WRIGHT

MAVERICK ARCHITECT

FRANCES A. DAVIS

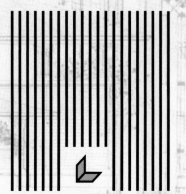

LERNER PUBLICATIONS COMPANY
MINNEAPOLIS

To Earl

I would like to thank Bruce Brooks Pfeiffer, archivist for the Frank Lloyd Wright Foundation, for giving me access to the microfiche at Taliesin West and for agreeing to be interviewed. I am also grateful to Win De Wit and his staff of the Getty Museum and Archives; Jack Holtzman and Dr. H. Nicholas Muller III of the State Historical Society of Wisconsin; and the Marchand Library of Princeton University.

Early on, Linda Goldstein, director of Woodlawn Plantation and the Pope-Leighy house, was important to me for encouragement and information. Loren Pope, the original owner of the Pope-Leighy house, graciously allowed me to tape his interview. Other help came from Linda Waggoner of Fallingwater and the guides of public Frank Lloyd Wright sites, particularly the staff of the Frank Lloyd Wright Home and Studio and the numerous owners of Frank Lloyd Wright homes.

I also wish to thank the many SCBWI-Carolinas friends who encouraged me, especially William H. Hooks, children's writer, and Jane Mruczek, former SCBWI regional advisor; Becka McKay, my editor; and last, but not least, Earl L. Davis who shared my interest in Wright and drove 17,000 miles in 15 states to visit and photograph Wright sites.

Lerner Publications Company
A division of Lerner Publishing Group
241 First Avenue North
Minneapolis, MN 55401 U.S.A.

Website address: www.lernerbooks.com

Library of Congress Cataloging-in-Publication Data

Davis, Frances R. A.
    Frank Lloyd Wright : maverick architect / Frances A. Davis
    p.   cm.
    Includes bibliographical references and index.
    Summary: A biography of the innovative American architect whose ideas influenced the direction of design in the twentieth century.
    ISBN 0-8225-4953-0 (lib. bdg. : alk. paper)
    1. Wright, Frank Lloyd, 1867–1959—Juvenile literature. 2. Architects—United States—Biography—Juvenile literature. [1. Wright, Frank Lloyd, 1867–1959. 2. Architects.] I. Title.
NA737.W7D34   1996
720'.92—dc20   96-12453

Manufactured in the United States of America
2 3 4 5 6 7 – JR – 06 05 04 03 02 01

Contents

Bear Run, Pennsylvania—the site of Fallingwater, one of Frank Lloyd Wright's most famous buildings

ONE

Home and Family

1867–1877

In December 1934, well-known architect Frank Lloyd Wright traveled to Pittsburgh to consult with department store magnate Edgar J. Kaufmann. Kaufmann, called E. J., was considering having Frank design a new office building. While in Pittsburgh, Frank traveled with E. J. and his wife, Liliane, to their vacation home at Bear Run in the Pennsylvania mountains. The Kaufmanns wanted a new cottage on the property. Frank and E. J. walked through the woods and tramped over ravines, searching for a site for the new cottage. As they stood over a waterfall on the property, Frank asked E. J. where he and his wife, Liliane, liked to sit to watch the falls. E. J. pointed to a huge rock, a perfect spot to watch the water tumble down and rush away. Frank's mind began working, and from that moment E. J.'s cottage began to take shape.

Frank always insisted that he shook his designs out of his sleeve. But of course, there was more to his creations than that. He always visited the site and asked for a topological drawing and engineering plan. Then he mused and dreamed about his design, working out the structure in his mind without committing anything to paper.

While Frank was still musing on the design for the Kaufmann's cottage, E. J. became concerned. He had not heard from Frank since the trip to Bear Run. E. J. telephoned Frank to say that he was on his way west for a business trip and would stop at Taliesin (ta-lee-EH-suhn)—Frank's studio in Spring Green, Wisconsin—to see the plans. To the amazement of Taliesin apprentices, who knew Frank had not yet drawn up any plans, Frank said, "Come along, E. J."

Kaufmann called again from Milwaukee, about two hours from Taliesin. Frank hung up the telephone and went to the drafting room. He began to draw the first-floor plan, second-floor plan, elevations (vertical drawings), and the details. Apprentices sharpened pencils and watched in astonishment. Talking quietly as he drew, Frank explained,

One of Frank Lloyd Wright's architectural renderings of Fallingwater

"Liliane and E. J. will have tea on the balcony. . . they'll cross the bridge to walk into the woods."

Kaufmann arrived around noon. He saw that the house Frank had designed sat squarely on the waterfall. He reminded Frank that he and Liliane wanted to view the falls from the house. But Frank responded, "E. J. I want you to live with the waterfall, not just look at it." Frank described the house in romantic terms. He stressed the cottage's organic nature, the way it emerged from the ground, and its use of natural materials. He called it Fallingwater. Kaufmann was delighted with the plans. He told Frank to proceed with working drawings.

The terraces Frank designed for the cottage would be cantilevered—meaning that the long horizontal terraces would be supported by steel beams and hidden concrete supports on one end and would hang freely on the other. But the contractor (builder) didn't trust Frank's design. He was convinced that these supports would collapse and wanted to insert additional steel into them. Knowing that extra steel would add dangerous weight, Frank insisted on his original plans. He ordered Bob Mosher—the apprentice supervising the job—back to Taliesin and wrote to Kaufmann: "Bob's continuous reports of rejection of recommendations and your criticisms . . . prepared me for this final step which I had to take when I found steel had been inserted over my head. . . . Lack of confidence is only a mild name for anything like that regardless insertion."

In response to the delay in construction, Kaufmann replied carefully. Frank sent another apprentice, Edgar Tafel, to take over as supervisor. But the contractor still refused to be responsible for the supports without extra steel reinforcement. When the time came to pull out the temporary

The construction of Fallingwater, October 1936. Workers placed these wooden frames, called "formwork," for temporary support under the cantilevered terraces.

Fallingwater

supports holding the cantilevered terraces, Frank kicked them out himself. As he had predicted, the terraces did not fall.

The first child of Anna Lloyd Jones Wright and William Wright arrived on June 8, 1867, in Richland Center, Wisconsin. Named Frank Lincoln Wright, the baby joined Elizabeth, Charles, and George—William Wright's three children from an earlier marriage. The baby's middle name, Lincoln, was a tribute to President Abraham Lincoln, who had kept the country together during the recently ended Civil War.

The new baby's father, William, was a man of refinement, charm, and wit, with strong interests in music and books. He held a degree from Madison University in Massachusetts, where he passed the bar exam. But he couldn't decide whether he wanted to be a music teacher, a preacher, or a lawyer. In Wisconsin, he first served as school superintendent and commissioner of the Lone Rock county circuit court. William became known as an effective speaker. When the family left Lone Rock, William had just been ordained as a Baptist minister. He began preaching at the small Baptist church in Richland Center. One month after the Wrights settled there, Frank was born.

The baby's strong-willed mother, Anna Lloyd Jones Wright, came from a tightly knit family of Welsh immigrants. Anna traveled with them across the Atlantic Ocean and had settled with them in the rolling hills of Spring

Frank's parents, William Wright and Anna Lloyd Jones Wright

Green, Wisconsin. The Lloyd Jones motto, Truth Against the World, seemed appropriate for the loyal, deeply religious clan. The men in the family—all of whom were large and strong—worked as farmers, while their sisters dedicated themselves to education. Anna had taught school in Lone Rock. Her sisters Ellen and Jane founded Hillside Home School in Spring Green.

Anna Wright was determined that her son would become an architect. She placed prints of old English cathedrals above his crib. Although William Wright moved his family frequently, the prints were always hung in Frank's room.

When Frank was two, Anna gave birth to a baby girl, Jane, called Jennie. William Wright invested in a department store's music section. But William had little money or business sense, and the endeavor failed. The family moved to McGregor, Iowa, where William preached in the Baptist church. With five children to care for, Anna became extremely protective of her only son, Frank. She watched over his every move and either ignored or harshly disciplined William's children from his first marriage.

William could not make a living preaching in McGregor, so the family moved in with the Lloyd Joneses in Wisconsin for a few weeks. Sometimes during the family's frequent moves, William asked his first wife's mother to take in his three oldest children. He believed they were unsafe with Anna.

The family left Spring Green when William accepted a call, or invitation to preach, in a church in Pawtucket, Massachusetts. Upon their arrival, William learned that the church could not pay his salary. The Wrights moved again, this time to live with William's family in Essex, Massachusetts. Frank was five when they left Essex for Weymouth, Massachusetts, where William accepted another church's call.

Frank at age three

The cathedral prints still hung in Frank's room in Weymouth. He gazed at them as his mother followed her Welsh family custom of "reading time." She read to Frank from the poetry of Henry Wadsworth Longfellow and the essays of Ralph Waldo Emerson, building Frank's love of books and ideas of individualism.

Anna enrolled Frank in a private school when he was six. She believed Frank would get a fine education there, but he hated the school. He thought the other students in their expensive clothes were show-offs, and he found the change from homeschooling to a regimented schoolroom disagreeable.

At home Frank liked to draw and look at books. When he was seven, his mother introduced him and Jennie to a set of educational blocks called Froebel blocks that she had purchased on a trip to the 1876 Centennial Exposition in Philadelphia.

The Froebel set included colored strips of paper and wooden blocks. The instructions involved twenty lessons, called "gifts," which Anna went through with Frank and Jennie. The colored papers fascinated Frank, and he made geometric patterns with them. He felt the smooth edges of the blocks and used them to build alphabet letters and Roman numerals. He also modeled with beeswax from the set. The Froebel set helped Frank develop dexterity and learn basic mathematical ideas. Sometimes his mother sat and watched him play, as the lessons suggested. Other times Frank played alone, using the blocks to invent his own games.

The Fourth Gift.

Fröbel's Second Building Box.

Large Cube, divided into eight oblong blocks. — The points of similarity and difference between this and the Third Gift should be indicated. In Wooden Box, $0.30

Diagrams and Directions for using the Fourth Gift. In Wrapper, $0.30
See also HOFFMANN, *Kindergarten Toys,* etc.

Frank's mother gave him a set of Froebel blocks when he was seven years old. The blocks came with a set of lessons, called gifts, that Anna did with Frank and his sister Jennie.

Frank enjoyed hearing his father play the organ, piano, and violin. Music became an important part of his life. Sometimes he went with his father to the church where William practiced the organ. As William played, Frank worked the organ's bellows by pushing the wooden air pump handle up and down, to keep the air pressure even. He pushed and pushed and dared not stop. The organ sometimes roared, shaking the windows of the church. Once, Frank stopped to listen to a melodic passage. Enchanted, he forgot to pump the bellows. Then Frank pumped furiously, for fear the organ would stop. Tears streamed down his face. The music sud-

Frank at age seven

denly stopped. Frank heard the organ stops click and the keyboard lid slam shut. Frank, exhausted, stumbled home in the dark behind his father. Anna greeted Frank with sympathy, irritated with William for working the boy so hard.

When Frank was eight, he and Jennie sensed unrest in the household. They could hear their parents' angry voices at night. Anna complained about how little William earned and how much he spent. The church partially paid preachers with gifts of food. Sometimes dinner might consist of seven different kinds of pie. Anna also missed being near the Lloyd Joneses. Frank was her only delight, and this devotion created a rift between her and William.

In 1877, three years after the move to Weymouth, William's parishioners began leaving the strict Baptist church to join the more relaxed Unitarians. William resigned as a Baptist and through Anna's minister brother, Jenkin, became a Unitarian minister. The family returned to Wisconsin. But William had no church to serve there. He became a music teacher.

The family stayed in Spring Green with Anna's brother James until their new house on the shore of Lake Mendota in Madison, Wisconsin, was built. One snowy day, Frank followed his uncle James on a walk through the hills. They trudged up a gently rising hill, Frank trying to keep pace with his uncle's broad strides. But James's footprints were too far apart for Frank's short legs. Then Frank noticed some weeds moving in the breeze. Their graceful arcs made shadows on the snow. He wandered from the path to gather some. When he looked up, he saw Uncle James had reached the top of the hill, and he ran to catch up. The tall man and the boy stood gazing over the farmlands. Uncle James showed Frank the family farms and the little family chapel. He pointed to the tracks the two of them had made in the snow. Uncle James's came straight to the top, while Frank's meandered along the way. Frank decided that maybe this difference meant that he was more interested in the stops along the way than a straight path through life.

Watching Frank wrestle and play with his cousins in Spring Green, Anna decided that her usually quiet, bookish nine-year-old needed a change. She decided she would cut his hair short like the other boys and send him to the Lloyd Jones farm to work during the summer.

After the Wrights settled in Madison, Uncle James brought them a wagon filled with produce. Behind the wagon was a cow to give fresh milk for Frank, Jennie, and the new baby, Margaret Ellen, called Maginel. Anna put her plan into action. She cried as she cut off Frank's golden curls. But Frank was pleased. He was tired of being teased about his curls.

Hair cut, Frank kissed his mother good-bye and climbed up into the wagon seat beside Uncle James. He sat up as tall as he could, pleased to be going off by himself with his uncle. This trip began a pattern that would last until he entered the university. He would spend winters in Madison and summers with Uncle James and Aunt Louise in Spring Green.

Although Frank liked the farm, he hated farm work. The first morning, he awoke to the sound of his uncle banging on the stovepipe that ran through his small attic room. What a racket it made. And the sun was not up yet! Frank struggled from under the covers and began to dress in the clothes Uncle James had given him the night before—a scratchy blue shirt, jeans with suspenders, heavy socks, and thick-soled shoes.

Downstairs Frank splashed water on his face from a basin. He followed his uncle to the barn to learn how to milk cows. Frank thought the cow smell in the barn was awful.

Sometimes cows pinned him to the wall with their huge bodies. He had trouble keeping the milking rhythm when flies buzzed around his face. Frank swatted at them and wondered when he would be finished.

After breakfast Frank helped Aunt Louise feed the calves. Their jostling and pushing frightened him, but Aunt Louise showed him how to get them to suck milk from his fingers. He helped the calves learn to drink from a pail. With one hand in the pail, he offered milk to the calf. When he felt the calf sucking at his fingers, he slowly withdrew his hand. He felt triumphant until a frustrated calf kicked the pail and splashed milk everywhere.

After helping Aunt Louise, Frank worked with Uncle James at the crosscut saw. Frank bent and picked up sticks and carried them to the saw. Repeating this task over and over, Frank worked beside Uncle James until dinnertime.

Frank and Uncle James washed at the pump, then joined Aunt Louise. She had heaped the kitchen table with boiled beef, potatoes, carrots, turnips, homemade bread and jam, sorghum and honey, and green cheese. Frank sighed as he sat, almost too tired to eat. Too soon he saw Uncle James wipe his face and leave the table. Frank mutely followed him to the field, where he held oak rails while Uncle James hammered them to the fence post. Stooping to pick up another rail, Frank looked at his hands. They were stiff and full of splinters.

Suppertime finally came. Frank was hungry, but his stomach churned at the unfamiliar, greasy food: salt pork, smoked beef, fried potatoes, cornbread, cornmeal mush, honey, and homemade preserves. At home, Anna Wright gave her son balanced meals with no fried foods or sweets. Homesickness and sore muscles kept Frank silent during the meal. Just sitting felt good. But his rest ended too soon.

Uncle James stretched out his long arms and announced that it was time for the evening milking.

The rhythm of pull and squeeze seemed easier, but the cows were just as cantankerous. Cleaning manure off the udders disgusted Frank. He hoped that this was the last chore of the day. His hands ached and his back hurt.

Finally, at seven o'clock, Frank dragged himself up to bed—fifteen hours after the banging stovepipe had awakened him. His sore muscles made movement painful. A deep sleep came quickly, but at four o'clock the stovepipe knocking began again.

A farm near Madison, Wisconsin, in the 1870s. As a child, Frank spent summers working on his uncle's Wisconsin farm.

After a few days of this rigorous work, Frank decided he'd had enough. He trudged down the hill, kicking at the ground as he headed for the river where a ferry stopped at Spring Green. He wanted to go home.

Waiting for the ferry, Frank dangled his feet in the water. He still hurt all over, his hands had splotches of dried blood on them, and his clothes were soaked with sweat. Yet he felt guilty leaving Uncle James. His uncle could do anything— break colts, calm calves, and split wood in just the right place. He wasn't afraid of anything, and he never got angry. A sadness tugged at Frank, but he felt determined. He would make his way home.

Then Frank felt someone watching him. Looking up, he saw Uncle Enos, his mother's youngest brother. Frank liked him a lot. Enos wanted to know where Frank was going. Frank sniffled, wiped his arm across his nose, and poured out his troubles. Enos tried to make him feel better. He felt the small muscle in Frank's arm and shook his head. Holding out his own arm, he told Frank to feel its strength. Enos told Frank that his muscles would get strong, too, if he kept working.

Frank felt better. He walked hand-in-hand with his uncle to the farmhouse. Without a word from anyone, Frank climbed the steps to his attic room and fell asleep.

Frank as a young man

TWO

On His Own

1877–1894

Frank attended school in Madison. Although he was shy, he made one friend, Robie Lamp, a red-haired boy whose legs were handicapped from polio. Both boys took music lessons from Frank's father, Robie on violin and Frank on viola.

The two boys spent many hours in Frank's attic bedroom, marked *Sanctum Sanctorum* ("sacred room" in Latin) for privacy. They sketched, painted, and composed stories for the small printing press in the barn outside. They also read books together, such as the *Arabian Nights* and the stories of Jules Verne.

Frank felt the tension growing between his parents. He overheard their quarrels over his father's spendthrift ways. Anna was unhappy, and William distanced himself from the family. In 1885, William asked for a divorce. Anna told him to go. He left, taking only his violin. Around this time, Frank decided to change his middle name to reflect his Lloyd Jones heritage. He became Frank Lloyd Wright.

When Frank turned eighteen, he decided he should go to work to help with expenses. Anna arranged a job for him with Allen Conover, a professor who also served as superintendent of building at the University of Wisconsin. Frank did office work and errands. Conover helped Frank enroll in university courses in French, geometry, and drawing. Frank found the classwork worthless, but he thought the work he did for Conover was useful. Although it wasn't much, this was his very first experience with buildings. Already Frank knew he wanted to design his own structures someday.

When he walked near the university, Frank often passed the state capitol building to check on the progress of the new north wing. Standing behind the wrought iron fence one day, he heard a tremendous noise. The whole interior of the unfinished structure had collapsed in a puff of smoke. Dust and blood covered workers struggling out of the wreckage. Some lay unconscious. One man hung by his foot from a window.

As a crowd gathered, firefighters arrived. Men tugged at fallen beams to reach those pinned below. Women wandered through in search of loved ones. Frank looked through the standing outer walls at the collapsed interior. This disaster—caused by poor basement supports—made a lasting impression on Frank.

Still shy as a university student, Frank avoided dating until a friend asked him to take his cousin May to a dance. Frank nervously agreed, but he was unsure of himself and wanted to know how he should act. His friend told him to take May into the hall and dance without stepping on her toes. Frank, still uncertain, asked if he should kiss May. His amused friend replied that that depended on the two of them.

While at the university, Frank had his first opportunities to design real buildings. He heard that his Uncle Jenkin, pastor of Chicago's All Souls' Unity Temple, planned to build a family chapel at Spring Green. Jenkin commissioned Joseph Silsbee, a Chicago architect, to design the chapel. Frank talked Jenkin into letting him design the interior. The same year, 1887, Frank designed Hillside Home School, a boarding school, for his aunts, Jennie and Nell. The school was located on the family land in Spring Green.

Frank felt professional after designing the modest chapel interior and the school. He begged his mother to let him quit school and seek work with a Chicago architect. He argued that he was nearly twenty-one and needed real architectural experience.

Anna Wright believed strongly in education. She wanted Frank to stay at the university. She pointed out that Frank's father had graduated from a prestigious eastern college. His aunts had founded the Hillside Home School. Designing buildings could wait. Frank should get his degree.

Frank urged his mother to write to Uncle Jenkin. Frank's uncle knew architects in Chicago, and Frank felt certain that Jenkin would agree that Frank should leave home. Worn down by argument, Anna wrote to Jenkin. To Frank's disappointment, Jenkin replied that Frank would only waste himself on clothes and girls in Chicago. Defiant, Frank pawned a fur collar his mother had sewn on his coat and some books his father had left and bought a train ticket for Chicago.

Frank could hardly sit still as the train rumbled into Chicago. On the platform, he saw people rushing around in every direction. His first glimpse of electric lights dazzled him. Not sure where to go, he walked toward the city's skyscrapers—the first in the world. Much of the city had been destroyed by the Great Chicago Fire of 1871, and he knew these breathtaking skyscrapers had been built using the latest engineering advances in foundations and steel frameworks.

Frank stepped onto a bridge and watched a barge come toward him on the river. A loud gong sounded, and everyone else rushed off the bridge. Lost in thought, he stayed where he was as the bridge swung out and carried him over the river. The moveable bridge amazed him, and he marveled at the skyscrapers. He vowed to become an architect who would design new buildings for this city.

After three days of fruitless calls on architecture firms, Frank stood uncertainly in front of Joseph Silsbee's office. Did he dare go in? He knew his mother must have contacted Uncle Jenkin, and Silsbee probably expected Frank to call. He reminded himself that he had experience with university builders. He would go in to see if Silsbee had work.

Cecil Corwin, Silsbee's head draftsman, interviewed Frank and looked at his drawings. Suspecting that the young man was Jenkin Lloyd Jones's nephew Frank, Corwin asked if he was a minister's son. Surprised, Frank asked why he thought so. Corwin told him that his own father was a minister, as was Silsbee's. He took Frank's drawings into Silsbee's office. When he returned, Frank had a drafting job that paid eight dollars a week.

Cecil guessed that Frank hadn't eaten much in the last two days and invited him for lunch at Kingsley's, a nearby restaurant. Over lunch, Frank and Cecil discovered their mutual interest in music. When Frank described his seventy-five-cent-per-week room at a boardinghouse, Cecil invited him to live with him at his parents' home, where they could enjoy music on Cecil's grand piano. Frank moved in that evening.

At work, Frank applied himself diligently, tracing and copying Silsbee's curlicue designs until even Silsbee couldn't

Frank with his good friend and coworker Cecil Corwin

tell which of them had created a drawing. Frank tried to learn all he could. He found architectural books at the library and read about ornament and design principles.

Outside of work, Frank and Cecil went to restaurants, plays, and concerts. On Sundays, Frank attended All Souls' Unity Temple, followed by dinner at Uncle Jenkin's house. At first Frank felt shy among his uncle's guests, who included Susan B. Anthony, a women's suffrage advocate; Booker T. Washington, a black educator; Carl Sandburg, a Chicago poet; and Jane Addams, the social worker who founded Hull House, a cultural center for the poor. Frank gradually gained confidence and freely entered their conversations.

Frank also attended Unity Temple's young people's group. When the group planned a play and dance following their study of Victor Hugo's novel *Les Misérables,* Frank played the part of Enjolras, a soldier. He gathered together a costume, buckling a sword to his waist. The sword tripped him at every step. But because it fit the part, he wore it until the dance music began. Young women no longer intimidated him. Frank enjoyed dancing as much as he enjoyed drama.

When refreshments were served, Frank dashed across the dance floor to look for a friend and bumped headfirst into a pretty girl who had played the part of a peasant. Helping her up, he saw a bump rising on her forehead and apologized. He gallantly escorted her to her parents. They gave him a formal introduction to their daughter, Catherine Tobin. The Tobins invited Frank to come to their home for dinner.

At the Tobin home, Frank arrived late for dinner. Catherine opened the door. She was sixteen years old—four years younger than Frank—and a student at Hyde Park High School. Everyone called her Kitty. She was tall with blue eyes and curly copper-colored hair. Frank found a warmth in the Tobin home he had missed since coming to Chicago. After dinner, Kitty offered to take Frank to see a new group of houses in a fashionable district nearby. Frank was enchanted.

Kitty and Frank began to see a lot of each other. The Tobins disapproved because of the difference in their ages. Frank's mother also disapproved. She was not ready to turn him over to someone he'd known so briefly—the only girl he'd ever really dated. Anna asked Cecil Corwin to talk with Frank. But Frank refused to end the growing relationship. Anna contacted Kitty's mother, who agreed to send Catherine away for three months. The separation made the couple even more determined and committed to each other.

At Silsbee's, Frank managed to get a raise from eight dollars a week to fifteen. But this wasn't enough to pay for the theater and ballet tickets, restaurant bills, and clothes Frank believed he needed to maintain his reputation as a young man-about-town. Frank had also left debts in Wisconsin. He briefly left Silsbee to work for another firm, but found that his skills weren't yet up to their demands.

Frank returned to Silsbee, who raised his pay to eighteen dollars a week. Frank still needed more. He wanted to move to rooms of his own. His sister Jennie now taught in Chicago, leaving Anna and Maginel alone in the Madison house. If Frank could rent a place for himself, Anna, and Maginel, they could all save on expenses.

Frank heard that the firm of Adler and Sullivan needed draftsmen to help with designs for a Chicago auditorium building. Hoping they might pay him more, he gathered his drawings and went to their offices.

At the interview, Louis Sullivan was surprised by the quality of Frank's drawings and their similarity to Silsbee's style. He asked if they were tracings. When Frank said no, Sullivan was impressed and hired him on the spot for twenty-five dollars a week.

Adler and Sullivan mainly accepted commercial, or business, commissions. Dankmar Adler, the firm's head, had an engineering background, while Louis Sullivan practiced the formal, classical designs of the Beaux Arts school that he had seen in Europe when he studied there. Beaux Arts building designs were often based on ancient architectural forms and included elaborate decorative details.

At first, Adler and Sullivan's huge drafting room filled with workers intimidated Frank, and he missed his friends at Silsbee's. Paul Mueller, construction superintendent, became Frank's friend. Before long, Cecil Corwin joined him at Adler and Sullivan.

Frank's salary enabled Anna to sell her Madison house and move to Chicago with Maginel. A family friend who lived in the Chicago suburb of Oak Park agreed to take in the three of them as boarders. Anna would work as the woman's housekeeper to help with expenses.

Frank had a closer relationship to Sullivan than to Adler—calling Sullivan *lieber Meister* ("dear master" in German). The two often discussed the future of American architecture after business hours. Sullivan was moving away from the Beaux Arts influences, and Frank was forming new ideas of his own. He believed that the United States should have its own designs instead of copying European architecture. His love of nature led him to the belief that materials such as brick, stone, and wood should be used in a way that emphasized their natural qualities. Wood should look like wood and not be carved like stonework. Neither should wood be covered by elaborate plaster designs. Capitals, or tops, on columns should be made of natural stone. Frank also thought that a building's location should be considered a part of the design. He asserted that all parts of a design—decoration, lighting, and furnishings—should form a unified whole, and that the whole should be designed to serve the purpose of the building's users.

Frank had few friends in the office other than Paul Mueller and Cecil Corwin. Some draftsmen resented Frank's closeness to Sullivan, calling him a Sullivan-toady. They often boxed for recreation in the back room after lunch, and they pressed Frank to put on gloves and box with them. Frank, who was small in stature, realized that the men saw his size as weakness and wanted to make him look ridiculous. He knew he needed to come to terms with these bullies. Although he had boxed a little at the university, he took a few lessons at a nearby gym to prepare himself. When he felt ready, he put on gloves and quickly dispatched his opponents. The astonished men meekly returned to work.

Frank assumed more and more responsibility for Adler and Sullivan's residential commissions. But he was still dissatisfied with his salary. He needed more money because he and Kitty wanted to be married. Sullivan told Frank that age twenty-one was too young for marriage, but he agreed to promote Frank to head draftsman, with a five-year contract at a wage above what most draftsmen made.

With Frank's salary secure, Frank and Kitty decided they could marry. Frank wanted to build a home for his new bride. He found a lot in Oak Park and went to Sullivan, to ask for a loan of five thousand dollars to build a small house. Sullivan saw the lot and agreed to the loan, but cautioned Frank to build modestly. He was familiar with Frank's expensive taste.

In 1888, Oak Park was a growing suburb. The increase of public transportation from Chicago made commuting possible. Prominent people in professions such as banking and insurance settled in Oak Park to take advantage of the many cultural events in the area. Frank wanted this kind of atmosphere for his family. He also thought that when he became an independent architect, Oak Park residents might be good clients.

The Wrights' lot was on the corner of Forest and Chicago Avenues. There was a small house on the Chicago Avenue side. Frank decided to renovate the house for his mother. He and Catherine could live there during the construction of their home.

Catherine reached her eighteenth birthday on March 25, 1889. She and Frank married on a cold, rainy day the following

June. Mr. Tobin wept, Anna Wright fainted, and Uncle Jenkin, who officiated at the marriage, cried as well. The newlyweds spent their honeymoon with the Lloyd Joneses in Wisconsin.

Frank remembered Sullivan's warning and designed a simple plan for a square, two-story, shingle-style house. To save money, Frank designed furniture that was built into the living areas of the house. In a corner of the living room he placed an inglenook, a fireplace with seats on either side, symbolizing the warmth of family life. Frank and Catherine moved into the house during the first year of their marriage, just before the birth of their first child. Frank Lloyd Wright Jr. (called Lloyd), was born in 1890. Frank had five Adler and Sullivan commissions to design that year.

Two years later, in 1892, a second child, John, arrived. That same year, Adler and Sullivan's residential commissions decreased, giving Frank only one home to design. To satisfy

Frank's Oak Park house as it appeared in the 1890s

In 1890, the Wrights posed in front of the Oak Park house. From left: *Jenkin Lloyd Jones, Jenkin's wife Susan, Frank's sister Jennie, Frank's wife Catherine (holding baby Lloyd), Anna, Frank's sister Maginel, Frank, and Jenkin's daughter Mary*

his urge to create new designs and to earn extra money to pay off his loan to Sullivan, Frank "moonlighted"—taking on projects outside of his work for Adler and Sullivan. He designed seven residences and one remodeling project, working at night in his home office.

In 1894, Frank and Kitty's first daughter, Catherine II, was born. By now Frank was ready to pay off his loan from Sullivan. But when he tried to do so, Sullivan told him that the moonlighting voided their contract. He called the houses bootlegged, or unlawful, and withheld the deed to Frank's house. In anger, Frank left the firm and severed relations with Sullivan.

The dining room of the Susan Lawrence Dana house in Springfield, Illinois. Frank designed this home in 1900.

THREE

A New Architecture for the Prairie

1894–1905

After leaving Adler and Sullivan, Frank opened a business office in Chicago's Shiller Building and did his designing at home. His first commission as an independent architect was the William Winslow residence in River Forest, Illinois. The formally designed front of this house contrasted with a series of windows, porches, and decks at the rear, indicating this was a home for the family to enjoy.

To publicize his work and boost his salary, Frank began to exhibit designs, write articles, and give lectures. The year after his break with Sullivan, he exhibited at the Chicago Architectural Club and gave a lecture at Hull House. In "The Architect and the Machine," he discussed the differences between mere houses and homes. He wrote: "Too many houses are like . . . bazaars and junk shops. Simplicity and repose are ideas to cleave to . . . something with a graceful sense of beauty in its utility from which . . . all that is meaningless has been eliminated."

By 1895, Frank's clients William Winslow and Chauncey Williams founded the publishing firm of Auvergne Press.

Frank designed the title page for their first book and did pen-and-ink drawings for the second.

Besides designing for Auvergne, Frank had eleven commissions in 1895. Frank and Catherine's son David was born that year, and with four children, the house became crowded. For Frank, who loved to rearrange furniture and try new ideas, this was an opportunity to design and build additions to the house. In a sense, the house in Oak Park became a laboratory for Frank's experiments with design and construction.

Frank designed a two-story wing to add onto the east side of the house. The second bedroom, which had been Frank's studio, was divided into two bedrooms for the chil-

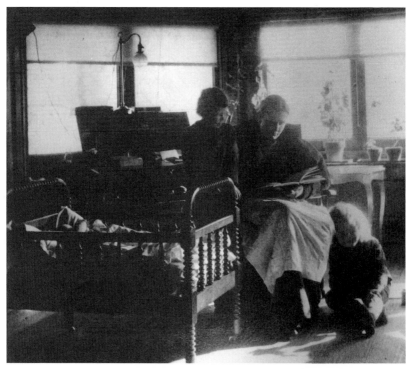

Catherine and the children in 1895

The playroom of the Oak Park house (above) *became one of the Wrights' favorite places for entertaining and relaxing.*

dren. The old dining room became a study, and Frank added a new dining room for the entertaining Catherine did to develop Frank's business contacts. Above the dining table, Frank placed an intricately carved wooden screen. When lit from above, the screen cast patterned shadows onto the table. Sometimes Frank or the children placed fallen leaves in the screen and surprised diners with the patterns on the tablecloth. Frank also designed the furniture for the room. A heavy oak table with high-backed chairs gave diners a feeling of enclosure, as if the table itself were a room within a room.

Frank also added a barrel-vaulted playroom to the second floor of the addition. The playroom became a popular area for both children and adults. Catherine, Anna, and Maginel all held parties there. Frank and the children used the playroom for acting out plays or giving concerts on the baby grand piano. To preserve the room's spaciousness, Frank had cleverly recessed the piano, building a wall in front of it and actually hanging the piano from a hook above the back stairs.

Frank connected his studio to the house with a passage built around a tree. Neighbors called the Wrights' home the house with the tree in the middle. The drafting room on first floor was ringed by a balcony on the second floor that had high windows to bring natural light to the drafting area below.

Catherine's entertaining made contacts for Frank that brought him commissions. But as the Wrights became a popular young couple in the community, they spent more money than Frank made. He continued to wear fashionable clothing and insisted that the children and Kitty have the best that money could buy. The older children each had music lessons—Lloyd on the cello and John on the violin. Frank continued to indulge in his love for the theater and concerts. The Wrights couldn't keep up with their bills. Still, their active social life paid off. Frank became established as an innovative architect in the Chicago area.

Despite his growing popularity as an architect, Frank remained aware of his responsibilities as a member of the Lloyd Jones clan. He participated in family discussions with his uncles regarding the aunts' management of their school. The uncles tried to keep expenses for the school within the aunts' income. In 1896 the aunts asked Frank to design a windmill to power their new water system. When he submitted a design, the uncles objected, calling it too elaborate and expensive. They asked a local contractor (builder) for an opinion. The contractor agreed that Frank's design was too expensive and said that it would not withstand the fierce Wisconsin winters. With this information, the uncles tried to persuade the aunts to build more conservatively. Aunt Nell argued that she and Jennie did not want an ugly steel windmill that could be seen from all five of the Lloyd Jones' family farms. They wanted a windmill that matched the school building Frank had designed.

When the discussion reached an impasse, the aunts sought an opinion from Timothy, a local stonemason. Timothy knew the aunts were fond of Frank and tried to evaluate

Romeo and Juliet, the windmill that Frank designed for his aunts.

the plans seriously. Yes, he told them, this windmill would withstand the Wisconsin storms and winters. Aunt Nell made her decision. She gave the commission to Frank.

After the windmill was built, the Lloyd Jones farmers watched out their doorways during storms, expecting it to fall. But Frank's design—interlocking octagon and triangle— gave the windmill stability. The design suggested to him the name Romeo and Juliet.

The same year that he designed Romeo and Juliet, Frank designed the format of the book *House Beautiful* for Auvergne Press. The book was printed in a special limited edition of ninety copies. Frank also gave the lecture "Architecture, Architect and Client," reasserting ideas he had spoken about in "The Architect and the Machine."

In 1897, the year that Frances—Frank's fifth child— was born, Uncle Jenkin asked Frank to develop plans for a new church to be called Lincoln Hall. Frank designed an office-type building of several stories containing an auditorium, social halls and kitchens, plus a gym and an apartment for Jenkin's family. Space for a series of small shops on the street level would provide rental money to help support the activities of the church. The innovative design pleased Frank, but none of them satisfied his uncle. Finally, Frank turned the project over to an architect friend, Dwight Perkins.

Now well-established in Chicago, Frank moved his business office to the Steinway Building, where he established a joint office with Dwight Perkins, Robert C. Spencer Jr., and Myron Hunt. These men became part of "The Eighteen," a group of young architects who met regularly for dinners filled with lively talk about new ideas in architecture. Frank called them the New School of the Midwest, but they became known as the Prairie School.

One topic of conversation for the young architects was the British Arts and Crafts Movement, which paralleled much of their own work. Both groups emphasized simplicity in design and the use of natural materials. Begun in England by John Ruskin and William Morris as a reaction to mass production and elaborate decoration, the Arts and Crafts Movement stressed designs done by hand. One of its leaders, C. R. Ashbee, a designer of furniture, metalwork, and books, became Frank's friend, as did Elbert Hubbard, the leader of the American Arts and Crafts Movement.

Frank agreed with parts of the Arts and Crafts Movement. The use of natural materials appealed to him. He, too, insisted that a common design theme should connect a house, its furnishings, and its lighting. But he disagreed with Arts and Crafts supporters on the issue of hand finishing. He saw that machine work could create patterns quickly and cheaply. In fact, he felt the machine could end the overly elaborate decoration that he spoke against in "The Art and Craft of the Machine."

The Joseph Husser residence in Chicago, which Frank designed in 1899, was a breakthrough for Frank in the planning of interior space. In the cross-shaped floor plan, known as a "cruciform," rooms flowed into each other.

The Dana residence also had a cruciform plan. Built in Springfield, Illinois, a year later for wealthy heiress and political figure Susan Lawrence Dana, the residence was one of Frank's first designs with a two-story living room. A balcony surrounding the room gave it an open, elegant feeling.

The innovations of the Husser and Dana homes showed the importance of Frank's continued experimentation with both cruciform plans and two-story construction. A year later, in 1901, Frank designed the Ward Willits residence, the first

The Dana house (above) *and the Willits house* (opposite) *are both examples of the low, horizontal emphasis of the Prairie style.*

house identified by architectural critics as Prairie style. Distinctive features of the Prairie house were low ceilings, overhanging roofs, and an emphasis on horizontal lines. Furniture, windows, and lighting all reflected the home's design. While Frank's Prairie homes emphasized nature and the use of natural materials, they also used machine work whenever possible. Later Prairie houses were even more open than the Willits house, with screens instead of walls separating the rooms. This use of space was called plasticity. He wrote, "Now why not let walls, ceilings, floors become *seen* as component parts of each other, their surfaces flowing into each other."

In 1902, Catherine and Frank's sixth child, Llewelyn, was born. The same year, Frank designed the Arthur Heurtley residence in Oak Park. The Heurtley house had some simi-

larities to the Dana residence. In both houses, the mortar between the horizontal bricks was deeply scraped out, creating shadows that mirrored the flat surrounding landscape. Other similarities included arched doorways and hidden front entries.

In 1903, Darwin D. Martin (known as D. D.) approached Frank about designing an administration building for the Larkin Company in Buffalo, New York. This building was Frank's first commercial commission. A milestone in its use of space and innovations in worker comfort, the building had a central core ringed with five floors of balconies. Natural lighting came from skylights and high windows called clerestory windows. For this space, Frank designed the world's first work areas with built-in metal desks and chairs. Other innovations included toilets and toilet partitions that hung from the wall, leaving space beneath to facilitate cleaning. The building also had air conditioning and fireproofing. The Larkin Administration Building became a model for modern commercial buildings. Frank developed an international reputation for innovative factory and office design. The success

Frank's first commercial commission, the Larkin building, made innovative use of space. Numerous high windows provided natural lighting.

of the building solidified Frank's friendship with D. D. Martin, who also became one of Frank's most important supporters.

In 1904, a year after the Larkin Building was designed,

D. D. Martin commissioned Frank to build a house. In the meantime, however, D. D.'s brother W. E. Martin, whose own Wright commissions were under construction in Oak Park, began to lose confidence in Frank. Lacking supervision, Frank had gone seriously over budget on the construction of W. E.'s home and his E-Z Polish factory. W. E. was so angry that he warned others to be careful in their dealings with Frank. D. D. spoke to his brother, trying to smooth the way for Frank. But he also wrote to Frank, asking him to be more careful about staying within the budget and meeting his deadlines. Frank endured these suggestions, borrowed even more money from D. D., and continued to maintain their friendship and correspondence.

The year Frank designed the D. D. Martin house, Frank also designed a home for the Cheneys of Oak Park. Edward Cheney was a rather stodgy businessman. His wife, Mamah Borthwick Cheney, was a well-educated, intellectual, and independent woman who believed in equal rights for women and men. Like Catherine Wright, Mamah belonged to the Oak Park Nineteenth-Century Women's Club, a club that Anna Wright had helped found.

Frank's success began to wear on him. An avid automobile enthusiast, he sometimes relaxed by driving his yellow Stoddard-Daton roadster well above Oak Park's twenty-five-mile-per-hour speed limit. Neighbors watched him whiz by, his long hair blowing in the wind. They called the car the "Yellow Devil" and wondered why Frank invited women other than Catherine on his drives. He said he was taking clients' wives to see his houses. But because Mamah Cheney most frequently accompanied him, rumors began to spread that Frank was being unfaithful to his wife. In fact, his feelings toward Catherine had changed. With a family of six

As he approached his fortieth birthday, Frank was busier than he'd ever been with design commissions.

children, Catherine maintained the house, ran a home kindergarten, entertained, and participated in Women's Club activities. Frank, too, worked hard. Neither of them had much time for romance.

A 1905 fire in the All Souls' Unity Temple in Oak Park gave Frank the opportunity to design a new building for the congregation. He realized that the temple needed an area where people could gather on social occasions, as well as a sanctuary. He placed stairwells in the corners of the sanctuary, as he had done in the Larkin building. The stairs allowed parishioners easy access to and from the sanctuary's tiered seating. Frank's design—two functional areas separated by an entry hall—was his first attempt to move beyond boxlike forms.

Because the church had little money, Frank made the most of the group's funds by using steel-reinforced concrete for the entire exterior and stationary supports of the building. Besides being inexpensive, this new material could be shaped in any form Frank chose.

When Ward Willits and his wife suggested that Frank and Catherine join them on a trip to Japan, Frank quickly agreed. Like many Americans, Frank had become interested in Japan when he visited an exhibit of a wooden Japanese temple at the 1893 Chicago World's Fair. Frank encouraged Catherine to leave the six children at home and go with him to Japan.

Frank admired the simplicity and use of natural images in Japanese prints. He began to study and collect them. He presented himself as a print dealer in Japan and traveled around collecting prints and art objects. Catherine stayed at the hotel, writing letters and worrying about baby Llewelyn. The Willitses were so upset by Frank's neglect of Catherine that their friendship ended when they all returned home.

Frank returned to Oak Park with renewed energy. He was, however, uncertain what changes he wanted to make in his life. He struggled with an important decision: to seek more independence or remain married to Catherine.

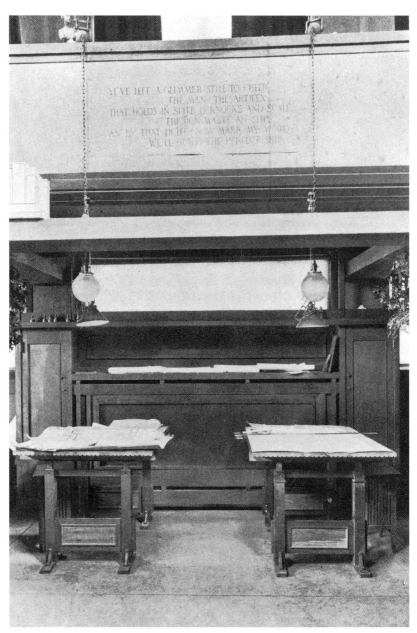

The drafting room of the Oak Park studio

FOUR

Conflict and Tragedy

1905–1914

Amonth after the Wrights returned from Japan, Frank and Catherine invited Unity Church friends to their home for a Japanese party, complete with kimonos, Japanese music, and Japanese food. Catherine also shared her trip with the Nineteenth-Century Club, showing costumes, art objects Frank had collected, and a model of a Japanese home.

Frank needed to interest investors in his Japanese prints. He was nearly bankrupt from buying art in Japan. He sold some of the prints, gave some as gifts, and used others as collateral on loans. But debts still plagued him. The sheriff called frequently to collect payments.

Frank completed designs for thirty-six buildings between 1905 and 1907. Among these were Tan-y-deri, built in Spring Green for his sister Jane Porter, and the Avery Coonley residence in Riverside, Illinois. The Coonley house had separate wings, each designed for the particular needs of the family. The Coonley complex also included a gardener's cottage and coach house, both designed by Frank.

The Wright studio ran at full speed. Frank was exhausted by work and by debts. His children were often underfoot, interrupting him during business hours. Catherine could not, or would not, enforce discipline. John Wright found a hidden stairway from the house to his father's studio. He led his brothers and sisters to the balcony above the drafting room, where they threw things at the heads of workers below. Other times the mischievous children listened in on their father's telephone conversations, sat on his hat, and drenched him with a garden hose.

Catherine Wright with Llewellyn, the youngest of the Wrights' six children

Although Frank felt nearly overwhelmed by his work, he still had responsibilities as a member of the Lloyd Jones family. One day, Frank's Uncle James was moving some threshing equipment to another farm. As James and two of his workers crossed a bridge with the heavy thresher, the bridge collapsed. The thresher's engine pinned the two men, and James climbed down to save them. He slipped and broke his leg. Carried home in shock, he died two weeks later.

To his grieving relatives, James's death was both an emotional and a financial blow. He had built an empire for the family by investing their money in land. Now, family members who had signed loans for land purchases were obligated to pay off these loans. Uncle Enos had to sell almost everything he had to pay off his debts. The aunts faced financial ruin.

Frank became deeply depressed and found work difficult. His relationship with Mamah Cheney had developed into full-fledged romance, complicating his emotional problems. He wrote to D. D. Martin: "It is difficult to square my life with myself. . . . My affairs are not in good order." His thoughts wavered between his long-held values of home and family, the unpleasant memories of his parents' divorce, and his deepening love for Mamah.

Frank's private life, however, had to take a backseat to his professional obligations. In 1908 he had eleven commissions, including the Frederick Robie home on a narrow corner lot in Hyde Park, Illinois. Robie, a bicycle manufacturer, approached Frank with exact specifications for the house he wanted built. He wanted to be able to see his neighbors without being seen by them. He wanted a burglar alarm and a fire alarm. He didn't want drapes or shades on the windows.

Frank placed Robie's house on a raised platform, elevating the living room above the crowded, busy street. The

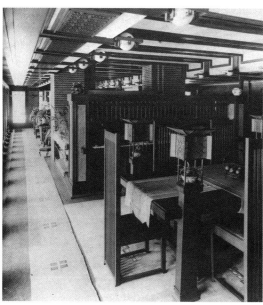

The innovative
Robie house
included interior
furniture and
stained glass
designed by Frank,
as well as Frank's
signature
cantilevered roof.

lower level contained recreation rooms for both adults and children. An outdoor playground surrounded by a brick wall kept the Robie children from wandering into traffic.

The most notable features of Robie's house were the Wright-designed stained glass windows and the twenty-foot cantilevered porch roof. The house also had a three-car garage, natural air conditioning, self-watering planters, a central vacuum system, and airy, spacious rooms for the household help.

In October 1909, Mamah Cheney left her husband, Edwin, and asked him for a divorce. Now Frank was forced to make a decision. He wrote to D. D. Martin: "I am . . . deserting my wife." In his struggle with himself, independence won out, and Frank asked Catherine for a divorce. Hoping for reconciliation, Catherine denied the request but told Frank that she would consider a separation after one year.

Frank knew the separation would not only create upheaval for his immediate family, but for Anna and the other Lloyd Joneses as well. He searched for a solution whereby he and Mamah could live together inconspicuously. By coincidence, Kuno Francke, a German architect and lecturer at Harvard, visited Frank and suggested Europeans needed to know more about his work. Soon after, the German publisher Wasmuth contacted Frank. Wasmuth wanted him to develop a complete folio of his work—a set of drawings, designs, and floor plans. Now Frank had an excuse to close his office and studio and travel with Mamah to Germany to work on the folio.

Frank thought his escape from Oak Park with Mamah was masked by the Wasmuth trip and that people outside the family would not be interested. He was wrong. People in Oak

Mamah Borthwick Cheney

Park had been following the Wright-Cheney affair for some time. Frank's prominence as an architect made him a public figure. A *Chicago Tribune* reporter interviewed Catherine, who stated calmly that Frank and Mamah were in Berlin. When a foreign correspondent for the *Tribune* discovered that Frank and Mamah had registered in a German hotel as Mr. and Mrs. Frank Lloyd Wright, headlines around the world screamed scandal. Catherine was again asked to make a statement. With poise, she faced a barrage of questions, saying, "My heart is with him now. He will come back, as soon as he can." She concluded, "When he does come back, all will be as it has been." In the meantime, Catherine had to deal with bankers and other creditors demanding payment for debts that Frank had left.

In Europe, Frank and Mamah divided their time between Berlin and a villa near Florence, Italy. Frank worked on the

Wasmuth portfolio. Mamah worked on a translation of a Scandinavian book on women's rights.

By the summer of 1910, Frank wrote to Catherine outlining the terms of their separation. The studio and home would be divided by a wall and the offices remodeled. Catherine and the children would live in the studio. Frank would occupy the original house on the Forest Avenue side of their lot for the time being.

Frank returned from Europe on October 8, 1910, leaving Mamah in Berlin. His homecoming was recorded by the papers, which noted his "smiling children." But Frank was not jubilant. He wrote to D. D. Martin: "I am not one to shirk responsibility for my acts. . . . I am accustomed to being alien but not to see women drawing their skirts aside as they pass."

In addition to feeling alienated from his friends and neighbors, Frank, as usual, needed money. He wrote John D. Larkin asking for a loan of twenty thousand dollars to buy out the first edition of the Wasmuth publication so that he could sell it in the United States. He also sent Martin a copy. He knew Larkin would probably refuse, but he counted on Martin to lend him the money. Martin did.

In the spring following Frank's return, Anna announced that Frank was building a small house for her on the Lloyd Jones property in Spring Green. She would live there part of the year, she claimed, but she and Frank knew the house would really be for Mamah and him.

Over the summer, Frank returned to Berlin to finish up his work for Wasmuth. From there he wrote to D. D. Martin and thanked him for his generosity. Martin wrote back, "What you term a fine nature . . . is commonly called a sucker." By that fall, headlines blared that Frank was still involved with Mamah. Catherine and Anna both denied these reports, but in December 1911, Mamah finalized her divorce and moved to the new house in Spring Green. Frank put up the Forest Avenue house for rent or sale.

The house in Spring Green was far from a modest home. Frank had planned a grand estate on the lands settled by his grandfather. He designed a drafting room, barns, and fields for cattle. Similar in design to a European chateau, the compound also included grape arbors, kitchen garden plots, and flower gardens. Frank called the house Taliesin, the name of a Welsh folk hero meaning "shining brow."

The nearby Hillside School no longer had enough students to sustain a large faculty. Parents withdrew their children because they did not want to have them exposed to the "scandalous" lifestyle of the Taliesin residents. Frank tried to

Frank began building Taliesin (above and right) in 1911. The balcony (opposite) provided a breathtaking view of the lush Wisconsin farmland.

save the school by making a formal statement in January 1912 that he was in no way connected with Hillside. Students continued to leave, however.

Frank found happiness at Taliesin. He hired a crew of draftsmen, including his friend William Weston. Mamah's friends and her two children came for visits. Although neighbors gossiped, Mamah's friendliness won them over.

At Taliesin, Frank continued to seek commissions, but they dwindled. In 1912 and 1913 he had a total of only six commissions. One of these was the Francis Little house named Northome near Minneapolis, Minnesota. This was the second house Little had commissioned from Frank. Situated on Robinson Bay of Lake Minnetonka, it became famous for its large living room.

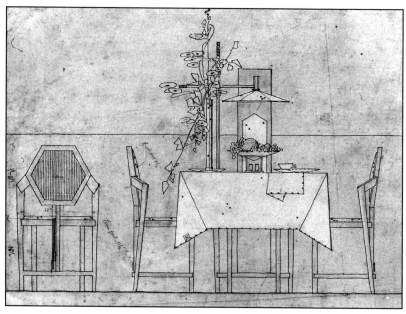

Frank was involved with every detail of Midway Gardens' design, from the furniture to the dishes.

Frank's friend Edward C. Waller approached Frank about building a palatial beer garden in Chicago. The hall would contain a restaurant, a bar, and a stage. Frank was skeptical, but the idea intrigued him. When Waller left Frank's office, Waller wasn't sure Frank would take the project. But when he returned later to give Frank a land survey, he found the architect already busy with preliminary plans. "I knew it," Waller said. "You could do it and *this is it.*"

The ornate design of Midway Gardens, as the project was called, signaled a change in Frank's designs. New ideas had

Some details of Midway Gardens, such as the ornately decorated concrete exterior, signaled a change in Frank's style.

emerged from his exposure to European architecture, Japanese design, and pictures he had seen of Mayan ruins in Central America. Although Frank's tremendous ego refused to acknowledge any of these influences, often an Asian turn to a roof or a feeling of Mayan strength began to show in his work.

Frank felt enthusiastic about Midway during construction. He had a large crew of workers, artisans, and artists under his direction. John Wright supervised some of the mural painting. Frank's old friend Paul Mueller signed on as a contractor. By the summer of 1914, workers were furiously trying to finish construction for the project's grand opening.

As Frank was eating his lunch one day, watching John finish a mural, a secretary burst into the room with terrible news. Taliesin was on fire.

Frank and John rushed to the train station. John arranged for a private compartment. Unknown to the Wrights, Edwin Cheney was riding on the same train. His children were visiting their mother at Taliesin.

When they all finally arrived, they discovered that seven bodies had been taken to Frank's sister's house, Tan-y-deri. The dead included Mamah, her two children, and William Weston's son Ernest. A butler named Julian Carlton was found to be responsible for setting the fire, but his motives weren't clear. Some said that he felt Frank had sinned by living with Mamah. Others said that another servant had insulted him, and still others said that he was simply insane. Carlton had waited until everyone was in the dining hall for lunch. Then he had locked all the doors except one, doused the rugs with gasoline, and set the building on fire. As people attempted to escape, he attacked them with a hatchet. William Weston had to step over his son's body to reach the garden hose and put out the flames before they reached the drafting room where Frank's work and his valuable Japanese prints were stored.

Frank's neighbors captured Carlton in the ashes of the boiler room. He had swallowed acid and was taken to jail with his mouth and throat badly burned. He died two months later, having never revealed the reason for his actions.

Stricken, Frank watched as neighbors carried away the dead. Edwin Cheney took the bodies of his two children, but before he left, he spoke to Frank. Without anger, the two men shook hands. Frank choked back tears as he tried to tell Cheney that he would rebuild every bit of the estate just as Mamah would have wanted.

Frank filled a plain wooden box with flowers from Mamah's garden. He and John placed her body among them. Workers helped carry the coffin to a horse-drawn wagon. John drove the team, and Frank walked alongside. At the graveyard next to Unity Chapel, Frank filled the grave himself and then turned back to regard the ruins of his house. He bowed his head in grief. He could think of no one except Mamah.

Frank at Taliesin

Shadows of Grief

1914–1923

Distraught and guilt-ridden, Frank moved into space in the Taliesin drafting room. Maginel, Frank's youngest sister, came to stay with him. She understood his grief and Frank welcomed her companionship. She persuaded him to saddle Kaiser, his favorite horse, and join her on long rides through the Wisconsin hills. At night they sat in front of the fire and talked.

Because much of Frank's mail blamed him for the tragedy, he asked his staff to screen letters. He saw only letters of sympathy or those concerning business. One letter given to Frank came from a wealthy sculptor, Maude Miriam Noel. Originally from Tennessee, she had lived in Europe for several years and had considerable social standing among wealthy Parisians. The sincere tone of the letter touched Frank. He invited Madame Noel to his Chicago office.

Frank had a unique ability to charm both clients and social acquaintances. Madame Noel was no exception. They talked for hours at their first meeting. Frank marveled at her

Maude Miriam Noel

dark eyes and expressive face. He learned that she preferred to be called Miriam rather than Maude, and that she considered herself a liberated woman. She and Frank had similar ideas about an artist's need for freedom of expression. Her ideas reinforced Frank's own belief that, as an artist, he was not subject to the rules of society.

During Taliesin's reconstruction, Frank kept an apartment in Chicago. Before long, Miriam moved in with him. But Frank soon became disillusioned. He considered Miriam's capes, turbans, and jewelry to be theatrical and inappropriate. Her moodiness frustrated him. Sometimes he found her in a dreamlike state, while at other times she was quite restless. He responded to her behavior with sharp and sarcastic comments. Yet in spite of their problems, Frank received loving letters from her. She addressed one to "Lord of my Waking Dreams."

When Taliesin reopened, Miriam lived there with Frank. When they quarreled, she would leave for brief periods. The housekeeper disapproved of the living arrangement. She gave a *Chicago Tribune* reporter the letters Miriam had written to Frank. She also claimed that Frank had violated the 1910 Mann Act by bringing Miriam to Wisconsin from Illinois. This federal law was passed to prevent men from taking women across state lines for sexual purposes. Frank hired well-known lawyer Clarence Darrow to defend him in court. Darrow arranged for the charges to be dropped.

Neighbors and relatives complained about having Miriam in their community, but Anna Wright stood by her son. Frank's aunts found that parents continued to withdraw their children from Hillside, and they closed the school. Frank, involved in his own problems, seemed unconcerned about his aunts' dilemma. He "bought" the school from them for one dollar and they left on an extended trip to California. Frank agreed to send each aunt fifty dollars a month, but he fell behind in the payments. Penniless, the aunts could not return home. Frank relented and loaned them the money, but he canceled his plans to buy the school.

In June 1914, World War I began in Europe with the assassination of Archduke Ferdinand of Austria-Hungary in Sarajevo, the capital of Bosnia. Before long, the Germans, Russians, French, and British were all at war. By 1915, Americans concerned that they would be drawn into the war grew cautious about spending money on new houses. The building industry went into a slump. Frank was even less likely to get commissions than other architects because of the notoriety surrounding his divorce and Mamah's death.

Bit by bit, however, Frank began to receive commissions. One came from Sherman M. Booth for the Ravine Bluffs residential development in Glencoe, Illinois. Frank designed Prairie-style houses for this planned community. Another residential commission came from Emil Bach of Chicago. The Bach house had a square, self-contained appearance that fit perfectly its location on a small city lot.

Frank also received significant news in 1915—he had been awarded the Tokyo Imperial Hotel commission. Frank saw the project as a chance to begin anew in a country far from people who criticized his private life. In December 1915, he and Miriam sailed from Seattle to Tokyo. With the support of Baron Okura, representative of the emperor of Japan, Frank worked on drawings for the hotel.

Guided by the emperor's art expert, Hiromische Shugio, Frank wandered about Japan looking for brass works, art prints, and ceramics. He planned to sell these treasures to American museums and private collectors.

Left alone, Miriam became either lonesome and clinging or bullying and agitated. One evening, she was so anxious and paranoid that she threatened to kill a friend Frank had talked with at a reception. When Frank became ill and Anna came to Japan to care for him, Miriam moved out of their quarters. She and Anna fought and refused to live under the same roof.

Frank's eldest son, Lloyd, became Frank's construction assistant. Soil samples they took at the construction site indicated a sea of mud lay under six to eight feet of top soil. Because of the constant threat of earthquakes in Japan, Frank

Frank was delighted to receive the Imperial Hotel commission in Tokyo in 1915.

and Lloyd did tests to decide on the best type of foundation to support the hotel. When Frank was convinced the foundations would be secure, he designed pillars tapered like ice-cream cones for a floating foundation over the mud. He designed flexible plumbing and electrical connectors so that the building could move during an earthquake without power outages or broken pipes.

Frank designed the Imperial Hotel in an **H** shape. The lobby, kitchen, and dining room were in the center, and guest rooms lined two long corridors on each side. Frank used carved lava, a soft stone native to Japan, for decoration. He wanted to give the building a Japanese feeling combined with Western construction methods.

While Frank worked on the Imperial Hotel, he accepted both Japanese and American commissions. He opened a business office in Los Angeles and shuttled back and forth from his work in Japan to his work in California. One important Los Angeles project was for Aline Barnsdall, a wealthy oil heiress. Her plans included a main residence, a kindergarten, a theater, and studio residences, all to be built on her property, Olive Hill, overlooking Los Angeles.

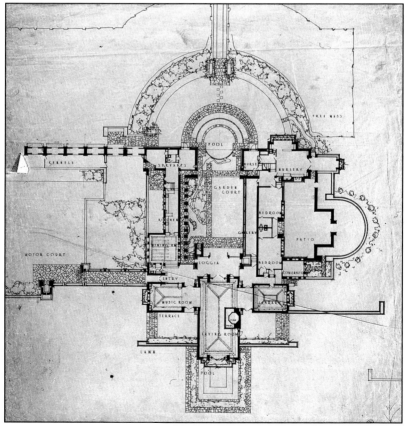

One of Frank's plans for Hollyhock, the sprawling Los Angeles estate he designed for wealthy heiress Aline Barnsdall

Frank was especially enthusiastic about designing the theater. Louis Sullivan had designed several theaters, and Frank thought this made him an expert on theater design himself. So when Norman Bel Geddes, the scene director of Barnsdall's theater company, met with Frank to discuss the project, Frank was arrogant and condescending. The theater was never constructed. Barnsdall relied on Geddes's advice, and Frank could not work with Geddes.

Frank did, however, make extensive plans for the complex on Olive Hill. Hollyhock House, where Barnsdall and her daughter, Sugar Top, would live, sat at the crown of the hill.

Barnsdall and Frank tried to meet when he made trips back from Japan, but they usually missed connections. Aline Barnsdall was restless and seemed to travel constantly. Frank didn't trust her contractor. Her business advisor didn't trust Frank. In fact, nobody on Barnsdall's staff trusted Frank. Barnsdall and Frank both became frustrated with the project. By the time it was completed, Barnsdall had tired of Frank and the whole idea of the complex. She lived in the residence for five years, then gave it to the city of Los Angeles.

By 1917 the United States had entered World War I. Most construction came to a halt. Frank finished only two of his American commissions in 1917, and between 1917 and 1918 he completed three residences in Japan. After the war ended in 1918, he completed a Japanese girls' school, Giyu Gakuen (School of the Free Spirit), and two more commissions in the United States.

Frank understood that following his six-year absence from his Chicago practice, he would need to reestablish his place in American architecture. He'd have to be more innovative than other architects. As always, when he had a new idea, he began to experiment. He developed a method of weaving concrete blocks together with steel rods and filling the empty space in the middle with poured concrete. He called this the "textile block system" because geometric designs decorated the exposed sides of the blocks.

The first textile block commission was for Alice Millard, an antique dealer. When Frank described the textile block system as fireproof, Alice was enthusiastic about trying it. She decided that her tapestries and artwork would be safely displayed against its walls. Because the Millard property had a deep ravine on one side, Frank designed a vertical house with a reflecting pool in the ravine. La Miniatura, the name Alice chose for the house, was like a miniature jewel. The house was exactly what she wanted.

But trouble awaited La Miniatura. Unfamiliar as Frank was with California, he hadn't known that the ravine, or arroyo, was apt to flood. After the house was built, the first heavy rainstorm filled the ravine. Water and mud rushed into the house, shutting down the gas, water, and electrical systems. After repairs were made, another downpour leaked water through the sunbaked roof. Again Frank made repairs, and Alice was finally able to enjoy La Miniatura.

Frank designed three other textile block houses in California: the Storer and Freeman residences in 1922 and the Ennis residence in 1923. Lloyd Wright supervised construction for these projects while Frank worked in Japan. Each residence reflected a theatrical mood, possibly a result of Frank's exposure to Hollywood film society while he worked in California.

Frank and Miriam returned to Taliesin in November 1922. Following many years of separation from Catherine,

This view of the Ennis house, built in 1923 in Los Angeles, shows the ornate detail of Frank's concrete "textile blocks."

Frank tried again to finalize their divorce. This time, Catherine relented and signed the papers. Frank and Miriam were married on a bridge over the Wisconsin River, at midnight. The marriage puzzled Frank's friends and family. Miriam was unpredictable, delusional, and dishonest. Frank even suspected that she might be addicted to morphine. After the marriage, Frank made arrangements for Anna to live elsewhere. Frank's mother and his new wife both had strong personalities. Jealous of each other, they battled constantly for power over Frank.

In 1923 Frank received news of the Great Kanto Earthquake in Tokyo. He was concerned about his friends in Tokyo but didn't worry about the Imperial Hotel. Frank knew he had designed a strong building. He also believed that if a building of his were destroyed, a better one could be built. Still, Frank was relieved when he received a telegram from Spring Green stating that the hotel stood undamaged. The pool in front of the main entrance had been used to extinguish fires, just as Frank had planned. The hotel's rooms had become a haven for Tokyo residents displaced by the disaster. An American engineer later reported that one of the building's wings had dropped several feet, the floors had buckled, and a connecting passage had been ripped apart. But the hotel's damage was minor compared to the rest of Tokyo. For years, Frank reminded prospective clients of his success in designing the hotel that withstood an earthquake.

The years 1923 and 1924 were unhappy for Frank. Anna Wright died February 9, 1923. Louis Sullivan died a year later. Frank had reconciled with his beloved mentor and was deeply upset by his death. Frank had no new commissions. He designed a sculpture and some commercial commissions, but they were never built. Yet Frank's creative spirit urged him on. He had to design.

Frank had difficulty obtaining commissions because many people considered Prairie houses to be outdated. The new movement in architecture followed the European Internationalists, such as Walter Gropius, who had designed the Bauhaus complex for modern art in Germany, and his colleagues Ludwig Mies van der Rohe and Le Corbusier.

Although Frank respected Le Corbusier and Mies van der Rohe as architects, he disagreed with the Internationalist attitude. In Frank's opinion, their buildings were sterile and seemed separated from the ground. He believed that houses should be united with their location and with nature. Further, he thought that all the Internationalist buildings looked alike, as if designed from a formula. They often had exposed gas pipes or heating ducts. Frank called this "indecent exposure." In response to the Internationalist claim of simplicity, Frank wrote: "Plainness was not necessarily simplicity. . . . To know what to leave out and what to put in, just where and just how, ah *that* is to be educated in knowledge of simplicity—toward the ultimate freedom of expression."

As the 1920s ended, both Frank's private life and his professional life grew uncertain. The Oak Park property remained unsold. He and Miriam became even more incompatible. He considered returning to California with the hope of being seen once again as a creative leader with a vision for the future.

Frank (standing) with some of his drafters at Taliesin

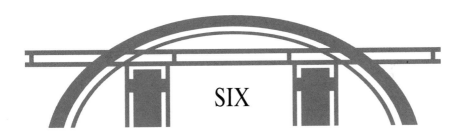

SIX

Disaster but Not Defeat

1923–1929

Miriam had always left Frank when they quarreled, but when she left for a long time in 1924, he believed he was free of her. Once his lawyers found her and she signed the Oak Park realty papers, he could divorce her. He could no longer stand her unpredictable behavior.

With both his mother and Sullivan dead, Frank had no one to turn to for unconditional support. He spent his days working and his evenings socializing with his draftsmen and their wives and with the workers who came to Taliesin to learn about architecture. Some played instruments, and Frank enjoyed hearing his favorite Bach, Beethoven, and Handel. Still, he had moments of loneliness and regret. He missed close female companionship. There had always been a wife, a girlfriend, or a mother near him.

One Sunday night in November 1924, Frank and a friend attended the ballet in Chicago. A graceful, slender woman was ushered to the seat beside them. Both men were impressed with her beauty. At a pause in the dancing, Frank made a critical comment about the performance to his friend.

The woman could not avoid hearing, and Frank saw her glance at him understandingly. During intermission, the two men introduced themselves and invited her to join them for tea following the performance.

Frank was eager to know the mysterious woman. At tea, he learned her name was Olga Iovanna Milanov Hinzenberg, called Olgivanna by friends. She was from Montenegro, a province in the European country later called Yugoslavia. Olgivanna was a dancer, part of Georgei Ivanovitch Gurdjieff's Russian Institute of Harmonious Development. Members of Gurdjieff's group practiced physical and psychological self-discipline. Olgivanna had joined the group in Russia and traveled with them to Paris. Frank asked why she was in the United States, and she told him that Gurdjieff's group had performed in New York. She was in Chicago with her seven-year-old daughter, Svetlana, to negotiate a divorce.

On his way home, Frank kept thinking about Olgivanna. Her poise and her melodic voice intrigued him. He was eager to see her again and did so during the next few days. He knew she would enjoy Taliesin's musical evenings, and he invited her to visit. When she did, the young people staying at Taliesin applauded her dancing and adopted her as their own.

Frank had to make a quick trip to California by train to check on his projects, but he returned to Wisconsin at Christmas to see Olgivanna. He was enthralled with her—and she with him. They took long walks in the fields surrounding Taliesin. By the time the New Year arrived, Olgivanna had moved to Taliesin.

The following spring, an electrical fire struck Taliesin. The telephone system that Frank had installed to connect his bedroom to the kitchen started to buzz and would not stop. Frank investigated and found smoke pouring into the hallway from his bedroom. The bed and the curtains were ablaze. Taliesin residents quickly organized a bucket brigade, passing pails of water and dousing the flames. The fire appeared to be out. But soon crackling flames could be heard within the walls, and Frank called the Spring Green fire department. By the time the firefighters arrived, windblown sparks had scattered over the entire house.

Twice now, fire had destroyed Taliesin's living quarters. These experiences only added to Frank's obsessive concern about fire. He always made provisions for water to be close to the buildings he designed.

Insurance covered some of the damage, but many uninsured pieces of art were destroyed. Frank immediately set to work drawing pencil sketches for a new, better Taliesin. He found pieces of broken pottery and melted bronze to mix into the concrete for the new building. Lacking funds as usual, he appealed to D. D. Martin. Martin reluctantly loaned Frank the money. Frank's words, said Martin, could pull money from a stone.

Although Frank had few commissions in 1925, he did receive good news. A Dutch architect and publisher named Wijdeveld wanted to publish a special edition of the architectural magazine, *Wendingen,* devoted entirely to Frank's work. The edition would be bound as a book and noted architectural critics would contribute essays about Frank's work. Wijdeveld himself wrote the foreword, praising Frank's dedication to architectural beauty and proportion.

Meantime, Taliesin was being rebuilt and Olgivanna was obtaining her divorce. Frank delayed filing for his own divorce because he did not want to upset Miriam until she had signed the Oak Park realty papers. When he did file, Miriam countered by threatening to publicly accuse Frank of physical cruelty. Frank withdrew his suit, but Miriam suddenly announced she was filing for divorce on grounds of assault. Olgivanna was now eight months pregnant, and Frank was eager to reach an agreement with Miriam. He offered her a handsome settlement if she would return to Paris.

But Miriam was not in a mood to accept the offer. She wanted Frank for herself. She followed him and called press conferences to complain of how she had been wronged. Newspaper reporters, sensing a story, filled the roads to Taliesin.

On December 2, 1925, Olgivanna had a baby girl, Iovanna. She was Olgivanna's second child and Frank's seventh. Upon

Olgivanna with baby Iovanna

hearing of the child, Miriam went to the hospital and caused such a scene that a tearful Olgivanna took baby Iovanna and fled to her brother's house in New York.

When Miriam filed a suit stating that Olgivanna had stolen Frank from her, Frank's attorney advised him to take Olgivanna, Svetlana, and Iovanna into hiding. Under the names Mr. and Mrs. Richardson, Frank and Olgivanna rented a cottage on the shore of Minnesota's Lake Minnetonka. Frank worked on his autobiography and enjoyed sailing, while a worried Olgivanna took care of the children.

Another blow came when Vlademar Hinzenberg, Olgivanna's former husband and Svetlana's father, found out that Frank and Olgivanna had disappeared. Afraid that his daughter had been kidnapped, Hinzenberg filed legal papers prohibiting Frank from taking her out of the country. Then he added a suit charging Frank with violation of the Mann Act. As a result, an all-points bulletin was circulated for the arrest of Frank and Olgivanna.

One day, Frank took Olgivanna and the children shopping in the town near the lake. Someone overheard Olgivanna call her child Svetlana and alerted the police. After verifying Frank's identity, the police arrested him. The whole family spent the night in jail.

The next morning, Frank posted bonds totalling $18,000 to get himself and his family out of jail. But their problems were far from over. Frank found out that Hinzenberg had filed a new suit charging that Frank had taken Olgivanna away from him. Miriam, meanwhile, was trying to have Olgivanna deported, charging that she had overstayed her visa.

By now, Frank and Olgivanna's affairs had been so ridiculously publicized that friends and relatives rallied around them. Catherine Wright even offered to help. Poet

Carl Sandburg, journalist Robert Lovett, and many others pressed the federal district attorney to drop the Mann Act charges. Hinzenberg realized that Svetlana had not been kidnapped and withdrew his charges. He and Olgivanna arranged for Svetlana's joint custody. Because the courts had closed Taliesin to Frank, he and Olgivanna went to La Jolla, California, to live in a rented house.

In February 1926, another electrical fire ravaged Taliesin, destroying books, blueprints, and drawings. To make matters worse, the bank—to which Frank was deeply in debt—sold the livestock and attempted to take possession of Taliesin. Frank persuaded the bank to let him raise some money by auctioning his remaining Japanese prints. The bank agreed, and Frank arranged a sale at the Anderson Gallery in New York. Frank obtained nothing from the sale, however, because he owed the gallery too much money.

Frank hired a new lawyer, Philip La Follette, the son of a famous Wisconsin politician. La Follette negotiated terms with the bank that allowed Frank to use the drafting room at Taliesin. La Follette also settled Olgivanna's deportation proceedings. Armed with the knowledge that Miriam's children from an earlier marriage had threatened to stop supporting her if she did not sign the divorce papers, La Follette pressed her to sign. She agreed to his terms in August 1927: $6,000 in cash, a trust fund of $30,000, and $250 a month for life. Frank also agreed to wait a year before marrying again.

In the meantime, Frank became annoyed by La Follette's suggestion that he and Olgivanna should not live together during the year they had to wait before marrying. Despite this suggestion—which Frank did not intend to follow—his life was straightening out. He was legally free of Miriam.

With La Follette handling the bank, Frank could begin

to act on his idea to incorporate his architectural practice—selling shares against future income. Shareholders would receive Frank's earnings and distribute them as they saw fit. They could then pay off Frank's debts and save him from further financial concern. He would receive enough money from the corporation to live on, but not enough for extravagant purchases.

D. D. Martin considered the idea of Wright, Incorporated. He said he would participate if Frank could find others willing to invest. Days after Frank's divorce, Wright, Incorporated, became a legal entity, able to issue stock and assume control of Frank's estate and finances. Frank's sister Jane, his friend D. D. Martin, and his attorney, La Follette, all invested.

The winter of 1927-28 brought Frank a welcome gift. Albert McArthur, a former worker in Frank's Oak Park studio, had started working as an architect in Phoenix, Arizona. He and his brothers, Warren and Charles, had plans to build the Arizona Biltmore Hotel, hoping to entice wealthy easterners to winter in Arizona. The McArthurs asked Frank about the textile block system. Frank responded by praising the system's efficiency. With his customary bravado, he offered to act as a consultant on the project.

Frank was elated when the McArthurs asked him to come to Arizona. He would receive one thousand dollars a month and a promise of fifty thousand dollars for the use of the textile block system. The McArthurs incorrectly assumed that Frank held a patent for the blocks. They also didn't know that Frank's son Lloyd had actually built the California block houses and had more experience than his father in producing the blocks and threading them with steel rods. After consulting Lloyd about the textile blocks, Frank and Olgivanna left the harsh Wisconsin winter for sunny Arizona.

The interior of the Arizona Biltmore Hotel. Although Frank was not officially recognized as the hotel's architect, many people believe that he designed it.

The official architect for the Arizona Biltmore Hotel was Albert McArthur. But many people suspected that Frank actually designed the building. Frank signed a statement saying that the hotel and cottages were McArthur's work, but the ambiguously worded document didn't really confirm the hotel's origin.

Frank earned enough money from his work on the Biltmore to settle with his bank. Wright, Incorporated, now had enough assets to resume ownership of Taliesin. Frank and Olgivanna married in San Diego on August 24, 1928. They returned to Spring Green.

But Frank had more work to do in Arizona. He was designing the San Marco resort for A. J. Chandler. After seeing Frank's preliminary designs, Chandler urged him to come to San Marco immediately. Frank, Olgivanna, and the children piled into Frank's Packard, and his "boys"—Taliesin employees—followed them in a caravan of cars. When the group arrived, Frank found that hotels were too expensive. He persuaded Chandler to let them build their own camp in the

Frank's plan for San-Marcos-in-the-Desert, an Arizona resort

Frank and his family at Ocatillo, the camp Frank designed in Arizona. From left: *Olgivanna's daughter Svetlana, Iovanna Wright, Olgivanna, and Frank*

desert. Quickly, Frank designed fifteen small cabins and the group started to build them. Red canvas covered cabin windows and ceilings. A rose-colored, jagged-edged fence—echoing the lines of the surrounding mountains—encircled the camp. Frank named the camp Ocatillo after a spiky cactus with bright red flowers.

Facilities may have been crude at Ocatillo, but Frank managed to obtain his usual luxuries. He decorated his cabin with Indian rugs. He even purchased a grand piano. By June 1929 estimates had been made, Paul Mueller had signed on as a contractor, and construction could go ahead. The

Frank, Iovanna, and Frank's "boys"—his Taliesin assistants—in 1930

Wrights returned to Taliesin and waited for Chandler to raise funds for the project.

While Chandler raised money, Frank worked on a home for his cousin Richard Lloyd Jones, editor of a Tulsa, Oklahoma, newspaper. As a relative, Richard felt free to argue with his cousin over the house's design. Richard complained that Frank was designing an experimental house and wasn't

The Tulsa, Oklahoma, house that Frank designed for his cousin Richard Lloyd Jones

paying enough attention to his requests. The two of them bickered throughout construction. The Lloyd Joneses finally moved into their new home, only to discover that the roof leaked. Richard's wife, Georgia, reportedly said, "That is what happens when you leave a work of art out in the rain."

By autumn of 1929, Chandler was ready to begin building San Marco. But on October 29, as Chandler boarded a train for Arizona, newspapers announced a stock market crash. Everyone in the country was affected by the crash in one way or another. Chandler would not be able to finance San Marco. Because easterners could no longer afford to winter in the West, the Arizona Biltmore went bankrupt.

Frank now owed another nineteen thousand dollars in Arizona, with other debts to pay as well. He was also unable to collect his fee of forty thousand dollars from Chandler. Although the stock market crash affected nearly every architect Frank knew, he was discouraged. The only encouragement he received was publicity about Ocatillo in a Dutch architectural magazine.

One of Frank's renderings of St. Mark's-in-the-Bouwerie, a New York City building that was never constructed

SEVEN

Free to Teach and Create

1930–1938

In 1930 Americans were still feeling the effects of the stock market collapse. Money was in short supply. From 1930 to 1934, Frank had no paying commissions except for a Dutch glass factory, Leerdam Glassfabrik, in 1930. He continued to work on his autobiography and a book called *The Disappearing City.* He also accepted speaking engagements. The lectures that Frank gave at universities brought the largest financial gain.

Frank gave a series of talks known as the Kahn Lectures on Art, Archaeology, and Architecture at Princeton University in 1930. Lectures included: "Machinery, Materials, and Man," "Style in Industry," "The Passing of the Cornice," "The Cardboard House," "The Tyranny of the Skyscraper," and "The City." In these lectures, Frank conveyed his heartfelt concern for architectural progress. Students viewed him as a pioneer in architecture.

For some time, Frank had thought about using Hillside School for an architectural school. He and Olgivanna developed the Taliesin Fellowship, an apprentice program that allowed young men and women to study at Taliesin. He sent

From left: *Frank, Svetlana, Iovanna, Olgivanna, and Frank's sister Maginel*

letters to friends and to universities describing his idea: "Three resident associates: a sculptor, a painter and a musician, eventually chosen for the work to be done . . . . An inner-group of seven honor-apprentices, having the status of senior apprentices or university professors and three technical advisors trained in industry will also assist."

Twenty-three young men and women, including Edgar Tafel, applied to be in the Fellowship's first group of apprentices. Tafel was determined to study with Frank Lloyd Wright, but tuition was $675 per year at Taliesin, compared to $450 per year at New York University. Tafel completed his application and enclosed a letter explaining that he could pay only $450. Two weeks later he received a telegram: "BELIEVE WE CAN MANAGE A FELLOWSHIP FOR YOU IF YOU PAY ALL YOU CAN NOW. . . . YOU MAY COME NOW INTO TEMPORARY QUARTERS IF YOU LIKE. . . . FRANK LLOYD WRIGHT"

Frank (seated) *with Taliesin apprentices*

When Tafel arrived at Hillside, he eagerly explored the dilapidated Hillside building. He first saw Frank standing on the stage of the assembly room. "It was like coming into a presence," Tafel wrote. "And what a presence he had. He shot out electricity in every direction."

With forty workers, Frank hurriedly prepared for the students' arrival. Tafel was quickly put to work whitewashing walls. And when the first group of students arrived on October 1, 1932, their rooms still needed doors and windows. William Wesley Peters, a tall, lanky young man, didn't think he could sleep without a door. He removed a guest room door from the main house and started carrying it to his room. Olgivanna caught him, however. She told him that one night in the open wouldn't hurt him.

Although commissions remained scarce, Frank continued to create ideas and solutions for architectural problems. By 1931, America's economic slump had worsened. The country had plunged into the Great Depression. The employment picture was bleak. After President Franklin Roosevelt took office in March 1933, Congress enacted three programs to aid the many Americans who had become destitute. The Civilian Conservation Corps provided the unemployed with jobs working on government land—payment included housing, clothing, food, and wages. The Federal Relief Administration granted funds for welfare. The Public Works Administration hired workers to repair or build roads, dams, and other federal projects. People whose hunger had forced them to stand in breadlines were desperate enough to welcome governmental help they might otherwise have refused.

Frank's first paying residential commission of the 1930s came in 1934 from Minneapolis resident Malcolm Willey. The Willeys were people of modest means, and Frank designed a compact, single-story, efficient house for them. He planned a central core for utilities and put the kitchen next to the living and dining areas. The homemaker in this servantless home could prepare meals and at the same time participate in family life. This was a progressive new idea in home design.

The success of the Willey house showed Frank the need for high-quality, moderately priced houses. Frank began to develop ideas about community planning. In his Kahn lecture "The City," he had prophesied that the city as people knew it would eventually vanish. In *The Disappearing City,* published in 1932, Frank explored the concept of planned communities.

His plan, called Broadacre City, envisioned broad, spacious, landscaped highways; hidden telephone and telegraph wires; airfields populated by noiseless planes; and gas stations that offered multiple services and came equipped with overhead gasoline pumps. The residents of Frank's imagined city lived in modest homes like the Willey residence. They had humane, community-oriented jobs, without the pressure of long commutes. Each home owner received an acre of land to be used for raising food. Neither suburban nor rural, the community included transportation facilities and zones for homes, farms, factories, and commercial properties.

Frank intended Broadacre City to be a model for the entire country, and some of his ideas were adapted by urban planners. On the whole, however, the plans never reached completion, even though a model of Broadacre City was

The model of Broadacre City, Frank's vision of a planned community

exhibited in major cities in 1935. Funding for the Broadacre exhibit came from Edgar J. Kaufmann, the Pittsburgh department store magnate. Frank's relationship with Kaufmann began when the businessman visited his son Edgar Jr., who was an apprentice at Taliesin. Angling for a commission from Kaufmann, Frank was a gracious and eloquent host. He was not disappointed. Kaufmann commissioned Frank to design a new office in Pittsburgh and a new vacation home for himself and his wife. That vacation home became the celebrated Fallingwater.

The Malcolm Willey house in Minneapolis had been a prototype of a new kind of house Frank wanted to design— an affordable, accessible house he came to call "Usonian." Usonia was Frank's acronym for United States of America. Wisconsin journalist Herbert Jacobs commissioned the first Usonian home.

Frank designed the Jacobs home in an **L** shape. He placed the work space (utilities and kitchen) in the corner of the **L.** From the work space, Katherine Jacobs could prepare meals while keeping an eye on the children playing in the living room. One of Frank's innovations for the house was a gravity heating system. This system pulled the cold air inside the house, down under the floor, and through heated pipes embedded in gravel. Hot air then rose into the house.

Frank designed a more luxurious Usonian home in California for Jean and Paul Hanna. Frank named the wood-and-brick house Honeycomb because he had based the design on a hexagon with an opening at the back.

The Hanna's builders, who had never worked with hexagons, had difficulty understanding Frank's blueprints. Frank

HOUSE FOR HERBERT JACOBS
MADISON, WISCONSIN

The Jacobs house, built in 1936, was Frank's first Usonian home.

liked to use his own units of measure rather than feet and inches. The twenty-five-thousand-dollar home Frank had promised the Hannas cost them more than thirty-seven thousand dollars, even though the Hannas did some of the work themselves. They complained about delays and Frank's lack of attention to the construction. Frank blamed his absence on an accident at Taliesin: he'd fallen from a road grader and recovered slowly, suffering bouts of pneumonia and phlebitis,

Inside the hexagonal Hanna house—another Usonian home—rooms flow into each other, rarely divided by walls and doors.

a circulatory problem. Senior Fellowship apprentices supervised the site, but Frank's absence was felt. As usual, Frank tried to make amends by flattering the Hannas, telling them he wouldn't have agreed to design the house if he hadn't felt the Hannas were unusually able clients.

While the Jacobs house and Honeycomb were on the boards, Frank received a commission from Herbert Johnson, president of the Johnson Wax Company, to design an administration building. Johnson thought his employees deserved more comfortable working conditions. He also thought a new building would be a way to honor his father, the company's founder.

Frank invited Johnson to Taliesin. He was familiar with Johnson's reputation as a strong business leader of a major manufacturing company. Edgar Tafel wrote: "When we heard that the Johnson people were coming to interview Mr. Wright, we apprentices went to work: windows were washed, the grounds raked, floors cleaned and waxed, the vases were filled with foliage." Frank served a beautiful lunch for Johnson. The two men spoke at length. After Johnson left, Frank announced to the Fellowship that they had the job.

Johnson wanted Frank to present his plans to the company's board of directors. Frank explained to the board how his design shut the building off from the surrounding poor neighborhood. The streamlined exterior had smooth, rounded corners—a design element influenced by the popular fad for aerodynamic contours.

To enter the building, employees walked under a large covered area leading to the entrance. The low-ceilinged entrance hall flowed into a large hall of work stations, each with

Frank (center), *Herbert Johnson* (right), *and Wes Peters watch as engineers test the strength of the mushroom-shaped columns Frank designed for Johnson's administration building.*

The interior of the Johnson Wax administration building, Racine, Wisconsin

a Wright-designed desk. Tall, mushroom-shaped columns gave the impression of a forest. The board approved the plans without changes.

Building was delayed, however, because the government agency that was responsible for building permits had concerns that the mushroom columns would not support the weight. But Frank was ready to start construction, and he began without building permits. When asked how he could do that, Frank replied, "We will construct until they call out the militia." To prove the columns could support the required weight, Frank poured one for demonstration. Standing the column upright, Frank had workers pile sandbags on top of it until it held a load three times heavier than necessary. Frank took great pleasure in kicking out the supports and toppling the column himself.

Johnson later commissioned Frank for a home outside Racine, Wisconsin, and still later a research laboratory near the administration building. The Johnson residence, called Wingspread, was the last of the Prairie-style homes. By 1937, smaller homes that did not require a huge staff to maintain them became popular. Wingspread had a large central living area with a huge chimney for four separate fireplaces. Four wings led from this area: the children's rooms, the master bedroom, the guest wing, and the kitchen and servant wing.

The winter after he designed Wingspread, Frank experienced a second bout of pneumonia and phlebitis. He and Olgivanna began to think about wintering in Arizona, where the dry heat would be better for his lungs. When Frank's former client A. J. Chandler suggested that the Fellowship come to Arizona as well, the Wrights arranged a trek west. Frank bought 800 acres of land outside of Scottsdale, Arizona, on the southern slope of the McDowell Mountains.

The Fellowship traveled west in a caravan of vehicles, buying gas wholesale and stopping at friends' homes or camping along the way. Frank bought a pickup truck and had it converted into a mobile kitchen known to all as the Dinky Diner. Mable, the cook, prepared picnics for the group.

Functioning just as it had at Ocatillo, the Taliesin West Fellowship designed and built a desert camp. The camp's design mirrored the angular shapes of the distant mountains. The drafting room was covered with canvas attached to a redwood framework. When the canvas frames were opened on fair days, birds could fly straight through the building.

Frank built Taliesin West (above and opposite) *in the Arizona desert.*

The Fellowship apprentices also planted desert gardens and constructed a large triangular pool—for beauty and fire protection.

Frank capitalized on his triumphs of Fallingwater and the Johnson building by spreading his ideas through exhibits and publications. An excellent lecturer who could be counted on to deliver challenging remarks, Frank received many speaking requests. Architectural societies in Germany, Brazil, and Belgium granted him honorary membership. An exhibit celebrating his work traveled through Europe and the United States. His 1932 autobiography and other writings enhanced his reputation all over the world.

Frank and Olgivanna

EIGHT

Crowning
Achievements

1938–1959

Wright first learned of Ludd Myrl Spivey when a telegram arrived at Taliesin in 1938, asking Frank to wire collect when and where they could meet. Spivey was the public relations–minded president of a nearly bankrupt college in Lakeland, Florida. He'd renamed the college Florida Southern College in 1925, hoping to attract new donors. He thought a new campus would help the institution recover physically and financially.

Frank invited Spivey to Spring Green. The two men delighted each other with their enthusiastic ideas for the college. They had similar personalities and a similar determination in their work. Like Frank, whose tenacity in seeking clients was well known, Spivey was willing to go to great lengths to find donors for his college. Gambling that Spivey would find the funds, Frank agreed to develop a design for the college.

By September, plans for the college were underway. When the plans for eleven buildings with connecting walkways was completed, Frank told Spivey, "What I am most proud of having done in this effort is to have succeeded in making all units into the one gracious pattern—a complete whole for college work."

The chapel was the first building constructed, and eventually ten of the eighteen structures Frank designed were built. Students did much of the work, pouring concrete into forms and making each block by hand. The students were careless, however, about mixing the proper amounts of sand and cement and weaving the steel bars through the blocks as directed. Consequently, the early buildings were not well built. Frank eventually sent Kenneth Lockhart, a senior Fellowship apprentice, to live at the college and supervise construction.

The following year, Frank designed a multiple-unit housing project for the U.S. government. The government canceled the project, located in Pittsfield, Massachusetts, following protests that a local architect should have received the commission. But soon Frank had an opportunity to build the plans anyway, calling them Suntop Homes. Located in suburban Ardmore, Pennsylvania, each building housed four families under one roof. All family entrances were private, and each split-level home included a basement and a sunroof.

Frank's multiple housing designs and his use of prefabrication—the use of partially constructed materials—showed the public that he could design homes for families with considerably lower incomes than wealthy clients such as the Johnsons and Kaufmanns. In 1940 he generated further interest in moderately priced housing with an exhibit of a Usonian home at the Museum of Modern Art in New York City.

After reading Frank's autobiography and seeing the Usonian model, a young Washington newspaper reporter named Loren Pope wrote to Frank, asking if the architect could build a house for Pope's family for less than six thousand dollars. To Pope's surprise, Frank wrote back, declaring that he was ready to build the Popes a house.

Built of cypress wood, brick, and plate glass, the house included Wright-designed furnishings. These furnishings, built of plywood, were modular, meaning they could be used in multiple ways.

The Popes' small house eventually cost seven thousand dollars because of a rise in the cost of building materials, but

The Pope house illustrated Frank's concept of the modern Usonian home. Tall glass doors let light filtering through the trees into the living room.

the family loved their new home. Mrs. Pope could watch their two children play outdoors while she prepared meals in the work space or washed clothes in the Bendix washer, the first automatic washer designed for home use. Floor-to-ceiling doors in the dining area opened onto a garden.

Also in 1940, Frank received an unusual commission from C. Leigh Stevens of Yemasee, South Carolina. Stevens wanted Frank to design buildings for a plantation called Auldbrass on the Combahee River. Frank's designs included a residence, barns, stables, kennels, and an aviary (birdhouse). The layout reflected the odd, organic structure of the plantation's live oak trees. He wrote: "Each of its separate structures is laid out on a gridiron of hexagons four feet in diameter, with walls rising not in a true vertical of ninety degrees . . . but at an angle of eighty-one degrees."

Although Frank managed to finish projects already started, including the Pope and Stevens commissions and ten other residences, his work was interrupted in early December 1941. The Japanese attacked the U.S. naval base in Pearl Harbor, Hawaii. In response, the United States entered World War II, which had been raging in Europe since 1939. By 1942 a shortage of building materials halted nearly all construction, except for that declared essential to the war effort by the War Department. The shortage would last until the war ended in 1945.

Frank was a pacifist, meaning that he believed that no war could be a just war. He objected to the United States entering into a conflict outside its borders. He also believed that politicians, banks, and money managers encouraged war for their own profit, and his lectures and writings began to reflect these beliefs. The travels he had made to Germany and Japan—the United States's wartime enemies—

and the people he had known in those countries had influenced him.

When Congress passed a law requiring all able-bodied young men to register for the military draft, Frank fought to keep his apprentices. He asked the draft board to exempt them as agricultural workers, but his request was denied. Five apprentices became conscientious objectors—refusing to enter the military on moral grounds. Four of them—including William Weston's son Marcus—were jailed, and one was sent to a work camp for conscientious objectors. Frank came under suspicion of influencing his apprentices and workers. The Federal Bureau of Investigation (FBI) became interested in Frank's lectures about the war. J. Edgar Hoover, head of the FBI, asked the attorney general to investigate Frank's influence on his colleagues. The investigation found that Frank was neither a communist nor anti-American, and found no evidence that he was guilty of sedition (betraying his country).

Some men did leave Taliesin to serve in the military, however, and the Fellowship grew smaller. Despite the war, design work did not completely stop at Taliesin. Frank's only commission in 1942 was for the Jacobs family in Madison, who had outgrown their first Wright-designed house and wanted a larger home. After some experimentation, Frank designed the first of several solar-heated "Hemicycle" houses, in which heat was generated by sunlight coming through a concave wall of windows. In the rear of the house, Frank designed an insulating grass bank against the back wall of the first story. A stone tunnel led through this bank to the home's entrance.

By the 1940s, Frank needed a chauffeur. He had been a careless driver and had had several accidents. Frank enjoyed ordering the apprentices and other employees to accompany him. One day, just after the end of the war, Frank and his secretary, Gene Masselink, drove past a Lincoln Continental dealership on Chicago's Michigan Avenue. Frank cried "Stop!" With Masselink in tow, Frank strode into the dealership, his red-lined cape billowing behind him. He tapped a car on the hood and said that he would take it. Looking around briefly, he chose a second car. Then he turned to Masselink and told him to show the dealer what color he wanted.

Masselink pointed out the car they had arrived in, a bright red called Cherokee. This was the only color car Frank would have. Frank turned and tapped the roof of one car with his cane and told the dealer to take the roof off. He wanted a convertible. He then turned and abruptly left, leaving Gene Masselink and the salesman to figure out the bill.

Change was a fact of Frank's life. From new cars to rebuilding Taliesin, he was continuously discarding the old to create something new. He revised his writings as much as he did his designs. As soon as the first edition of *An Autobiography* came out in 1932, he immediately began to work on a revision. After the second edition was printed in 1943, Frank began changes for a third edition. Every time a new edition came into print, Frank's commissions increased.

Frank's designs gradually evolved from rectangular, triangular, and hexagonal forms toward designs based on a circle. Some circular forms first appeared in solar residences, such as the Jacobses' second house.

The Usonian house became popular in the building boom that followed World War II. Usonian houses were more affordable and easier to maintain than traditional homes. Women who had gone to work for the war effort sometimes wanted to

An aerial view of Taliesin as it appeared in the early 1950s, rebuilt after three fires

continue working. Most could not find, or pay for, servants to maintain the home in their absence. Frank's commissions ranged from Usonians, such as the Grant residence in Iowa, to complete community plans in Michigan and New York.

Lowell Walter of Quasqueton, Iowa, commissioned one of the more elaborate Usonian homes. Frank designed a large living and dining area, a broad roof overhang with up-turned edges to soften sunlight, and clerestory windows. Frank also designed all of the home's furniture, finishing it in rich walnut rather than the inexpensive plywood used in less costly houses.

An example of the interior of Frank's Usonian homes

In 1947, following the Walter commission, Frank designed three community master plans. The first two were located outside Galesburg, Illinois, and Kalamazoo, Michigan, and the third was near Pleasantville, New York. Except for Broadacre City, which was never built, Frank hadn't designed a community plan since the 1915 Sherman Booth Ravine Bluffs Development in Glencoe, Illinois. Frank designed winding roads on which he placed circular lots. The wooded space between these lots would be used as common ground.

The First Unitarian Society asked Frank to design a meeting house in Madison, Wisconsin, in 1947. This project was a special joy for Frank. His grandfather Richard Lloyd Jones was one of its founders. Frank's design placed the altar in an upraised point at the front of the church, like the prow

The First Unitarian Society meeting house in Madison, Wisconsin.
Frank designed the sweeping roof to resemble the prow of a ship.

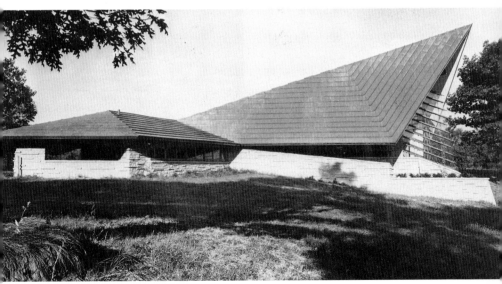

The V. C. Morris Gift Shop in San Francisco has a circular ramp inside—an example of Frank's continuing experimentation with designs based on circles.

of a ship. The two halves of the low, wide roof came together at the point and swept back and over the fieldstone walls.

The V. C. Morris Gift Shop in San Francisco was a rare commercial commission for Frank. He accepted it—along with fifteen residential commissions—in 1948. The gift shop's front, a circular brick design, partially closed off the entrance in an intriguing way that invited customers to enter. Inside, Frank placed a circular ramp leading upward.

One of the fifteen homes Frank designed in 1948 was a stone beach house in Carmel, California. Situated above the pounding surf of Monterey Bay, the house had a cantilevered roof and a circular living room overlooking the bay. Frank designed special living room windows to block out strong ocean winds, allowing only a gentle breeze to enter the house.

Although building Usonian homes was inexpensive compared to other kinds of home building, Frank realized that construction and labor costs had soared since the war. To lower costs, more and more owners were now willing to do part of the work themselves. After some experimentation, Frank designed lightweight blocks of precast concrete measuring one foot by two feet. Inexperienced builders found these blocks easy to handle. Grooved on the edges, the blocks could be stacked and connected by woven reinforcing rods. Frank called homes built with this system "Usonian Automatic." He wrote: "We have eliminated the need for skilled labor by prefabricating all plumbing, heating and wiring, so each . . . system may come into the building in a factory-made package, easily installed by making several simple connections provided during block-construction." The Benjamin Adelman residence, built in Phoenix, Arizona, in 1951, was the first Usonian Automatic home.

The Usonian's transformation into the Usonian Automatic showed Frank's ability to experiment and redesign. He often took ideas from his unbuilt projects and used them in new ways at new locations. Price Tower, Frank's fanciful design for a skyscraper in Bartlesville, Oklahoma, evolved from the ideas he had planned but never used for St. Mark's-on-the-Bouwerie in New York City.

H. C. Price, a successful Oklahoma businessman, had contacted Frank about designing a three-story office build-

The Price Tower in Bartlesville, Oklahoma, rises strikingly above the flat landscape surrounding it. Frank often recycled design ideas—the tower is based in part on the never-constructed St. Mark's-on-the-Bouwerie.

ing. When Price and his wife came to Taliesin to discuss the building, Frank convinced them that a nineteen-story tower was just what they wanted for their offices. With his usual dramatic flair, Frank said, "It will be like a needle on the prairie, a tree that has escaped the forest."

In the Price design, Frank suspended slab cantilever floors from a central shaft. During construction, the Prices' youngest son supposedly walked to the end of one of the slabs and started to jump up and down, as if he were on a diving board. The workers below scattered, certain the entire

Frank continued designing buildings when he was well into his eighties.

structure would collapse. Of course, it did not—Frank's cantilevers might have sagged on occasion, but they never fell. His engineering plans always provided adequate support. He'd learned that lesson when he witnessed the collapse of the Wisconsin state capitol wing. Frank liked to say, "If you don't learn by your mistakes, you are not going to learn anything because you learn nothing from your successes."

In 1954 Dr. Mortimer Cohen, rabbi of the Beth Shalom congregation in Elkins Park, Pennsylvania, contacted Frank about designing a new synagogue for his congregation. Frank immediately began studying American Jewish symbolism. The plans he submitted to Cohen incorporated many of these symbols. Frank envisioned the exterior as Mount Sinai built of modern materials: concrete, steel, aluminum, and glass. On the three ridges of the roof, he placed seven-branch menorahs, or candleholders. The fountain in front of the building symbolized the ancient custom of worshipers washing before they entered the synagogue.

Other large commissions that came to Frank in the 1950s were a theater in Dallas, Texas, the Annunciation Greek Orthodox Church in Milwaukee, Wisconsin, and the Marin County Civic Center in San Rafael, California.

In the early 1940s Frank had been commissioned by Solomon Guggenheim to design the New York Guggenheim Museum, a museum for modern art. World War II caused the first delay in the project, and after the war Guggenheim

The Annunciation Greek Orthodox Church in Milwaukee, Wisconsin—another of Frank's circular designs

Frank, curator Hilla Rebay (center), *and philanthropist Solomon Guggenheim stand before Frank's model of the Guggenheim Museum, a museum for modern art in New York City.*

waited for the price of building materials to go down. Then, a suitable location could not be found. Meanwhile, the New York building commissioners and the museum's director had grown skeptical of Frank's spiraling, circular design. Even Hilla Rebay, the museum's curator, began to have doubts about hanging paintings on circular, curving walls. Eventually a site for the museum was found on the east side of New York's Central Park, and in 1956 construction finally began. The design remained essentially the same as when Frank had designed it years earlier. Frank kept an apartment in the New York Plaza Hotel during the museum's construction, and he watched the building take shape.

Family and friends help Frank celebrate his eighty-ninth birthday in June 1956.

Frank wanted to return to Taliesin West for his birthday in 1959. The Fellowship always made elaborate preparations for Frank's birthday and planned to celebrate his ninety-second year on June 8. But he was becoming increasingly ill. Within the previous year, he had begun to suffer from Meniere's Syndrome, an inner-ear disturbance. The attacks of dizziness, nausea, and vomiting had become more frequent. Unable to always maintain his balance, he fell one day while in his apartment. On April 4, 1959, he was hospitalized in Phoenix, and two days later he had surgery for an intestinal obstruction. Although he rallied briefly, Frank died on April 9, 1959, of heart failure.

Architect and former apprentice Wes Peters drove Frank's body to Spring Green. On April 12 Frank's relatives gathered to pay their respects. On foot, they followed a flower-filled, horse-drawn farm wagon to Unity Chapel. Frank's body was placed in an unmarked grave a few feet from Mamah's grave.

Frank Lloyd Wright received many honors during his lifetime. Seventeen of his homes were designated by the American Institute of Architects (AIA) as buildings to be preserved as examples of his contribution to American culture. In 1951, *Sixty Years of Living Architecture,* an exhibit of Frank's lifework, began a worldwide tour in Florence, Italy. Frank received the de Medici Medal from the city of Florence and the Star of Solidarity, awarded in Venice, Italy, for architectural excellence.

During the 1940s and 1950s Frank published a number of books. He honored Louis Sullivan, his "lieber Meister," with a book entitled *Genius and the Mobocracy.* He also wrote several books detailing his views on architecture, including *The Story of the Tower, The Living City, When Democracy Builds* (a revision of *The Disappearing City*), *The Natural House,* and three editions of his autobiography.

Frank received gold medals from both the Academy of Arts and Letters and the National Institute of Arts and Letters. Several American colleges and universities, among them Princeton, Yale, and Cooper Union, awarded Frank with honorary doctoral degrees.

Despite the fact that Frank had never joined the American Institute of Architects and over the years had been quite critical of its members, he received their prestigious gold medal in 1949. Ironically, Frank cherished this award more than any other. At last, he had received the highest of honors from professionals in his own country.

AERIAL VIEW OF ISLE OF EDENA AND UNIVERSITY AT HEIGHT OF
PLAN FOR GREATER BAGHDAD
DEDICATED TO SUMERIA, ISIN, LARSA, and BABYLON
FRANK LLOYD WRIGHT ARCHITECT

Like the projects, large and small, that he designed throughout his life, Frank Lloyd Wright's plans for the Baghdad Opera were innovative and exciting.

EPILOGUE

Although buildings designed by Frank Lloyd Wright are highly valued, one in every six has been demolished or is deteriorating. Some Wright-designed buildings, such as the Storer residence in Los Angeles and the Richardson residence in Glen Ridge, New Jersey, have been restored by individuals. Other efforts, such as the restoration of the Dana Thomas house in Springfield, Illinois, have been funded by state governments or by corporations.

Architect Eric Wright, Frank's grandson, is helping to restore the Auldbrass plantation in Yemasee, South Carolina. The restoration follows Frank's original plans, and any new buildings at Auldbrass will be based on his ideas.

New Wright-designed buildings are also being constructed. For 20 years, Frank fought unsuccessfully for the construction of a civic center he had designed for Madison, Wisconsin. In January 1995, construction finally began on the convention center, Monona Terrace, located on the shores of Lake Monona in Madison.

The Taliesin Preservation Commission, incorporated in 1991, works jointly with the Frank Lloyd Wright Foundation to preserve Taliesin and 600 acres of grounds. Taliesin has been named a national historic landmark. Preservation includes everything on the property: barns, fields, the residence and its furnishings, collections of artifacts, even roads and ponds.

More than one-third of all Wright buildings are listed on the National Register of Historic Places. At Taliesin West, archives containing Frank's correspondence are kept on microfiche, and copies of this correspondence are also kept at the Getty Art Museum and Archives in Santa Monica, California. Collections of Frank Lloyd Wright materials can be found at several research libraries across the country, including the Avery Architectural and Fine Arts Library at Columbia University in New York City. His drawings are even available on CD-ROM. Because of these collections, as well as the Frank Lloyd Wright Home and Studio Foundation in Oak Park, Illinois, future generations will be able to explore Frank's structures and understand why Frank Lloyd Wright tenaciously held to his architectural principles.

Frank Lloyd Wright Buildings Open to the Public

Beth Shalom Synagogue, Elkins Park, Pennsylvania
Dana-Thomas residence, Springfield, Illinois
Ennis-Brown house, Los Angeles, California
Fallingwater, Bear Run, Pennsylvania
Florida Southern College, Lakeland, Florida
Johnson Wax Administration Building, Racine, Wisconsin
Pope-Leighy house, Falls Church, Virginia
Price Tower, Bartlesville, Oklahoma
Frederick Robie residence, Chicago, Illinois
Taliesin, Spring Green, Wisconsin
Taliesin West, Scottsdale, Arizona
Lowell Walter residence, Quasqueton, Iowa
Frank Lloyd Wright Home and Studio, Oak Park, Illinois

Sources

p. 8   Edgar Tafel, *Years with Frank Lloyd Wright: Apprentice to Genius* (New York: Dover Publications, 1985), 3.

pp. 8–9   Ibid.

p. 9   Frank Lloyd Wright, *Letters to Clients,* selected and with commentary by Bruce Brooks Pfeiffer (California: California State University, 1986), 99–100.

p. 35   Frank Lloyd Wright, *Collected Writings, Vol. 1, 1894–1930* (New York: Rizzoli in association with the Frank Lloyd Wright Foundation, 1992), 23–24.

p. 42   Frank Lloyd Wright, *The Natural House* (New York: Horizon Press, 1954), 45.

p. 51   Wright, *Letters to Clients,* 16.

p. 53   Ibid.

p. 55   Wright, *Letters to Clients,* 17.

p. 55   Meryle Secrest, *Frank Lloyd Wright: A Biography* (New York: HarperPerennial, 1993), 208.

p. 59   Frank Lloyd Wright, *An Autobiography* (New York: Horizon Press, 1977), 201.

p. 65   Secrest, *Frank Lloyd Wright,* 241.

p. 73   Frank Lloyd Wright, *Collected Writings, Vol. 3, 1931–1939* (New York: Rizzoli in association with the Frank Lloyd Wright Foundation, 1993), 324.

p. 73   Wright, *The Natural House,* 41–42.

p. 90   Wright, *An Autobiography,* 418.

p. 90   Tafel, *Years with Frank Lloyd Wright,* 16.

p. 91   Ibid., 20.

p. 97   Ibid., 175.

p. 98   Ibid., 176.

p. 104   Wright, *Letters to Clients,* 168.

p. 106   Brendon Gill, "Frank Lloyd Wright's Auldbrass," *Architectural Digest* 50, no. 12 (December 1993): 137.

p. 113   Wright, *The Natural House,* 202.

p. 115   Bruce Brooks Pfeiffer, personal interview with author.

Bibliography

Writings of Frank Lloyd Wright

An Autobiography. New York: Horizon Press, 1932, 1947, 1977.

Collected Writings, Vol. 1, 1894–1930. New York: Rizzoli in association with the Frank Lloyd Wright Foundation, 1992.

Collected Writings, Vol. 3, 1931–1939. New York: Rizzoli in association with the Frank Lloyd Wright Foundation, 1993.

Letters to Apprentices. Fresno: California State University, 1982.

Letters to Architects. Fresno: California State University, 1984.

Letters to Clients. Fresno: California State University, 1986.

The Natural House. New York: Horizon Press, 1954.

Other Sources

Curtis, William J. R. *Modern Architecture Since 1900.* Englewood Cliffs: Prentice-Hall, 1987.

Davis, Frances A. "Survival as an Independent Scholar: Frank Lloyd Wright." Paper presented at the first National Coalition of Independent Scholars, Bethesda, April 1992.

Gill, Brendan. *Many Masks: A Life of Frank Lloyd Wright.* New York: Ballantine Books, 1987.

Heinz, Thomas A. *Architectural Monographs No. 18: Frank Lloyd Wright.* New York: St. Martin's Press, 1992.

Jacobs, Herbert. *America's Greatest Architect.* New York: Harcourt Brace and World, Inc., 1965.

Kaufmann, Edgar, ed. *An American Architecture: Frank Lloyd Wright.* New York: Bramhall House, 1955.

Raymond, Antonin. *An Autobiography.* Rutland: Charles E. Tuttle, 1973.

Riley, Terence and Peter Reed, eds. *Frank Lloyd Wright: Architect.* New York: Museum of Modern Art, 1994.

Roth, Leland M. *Concise History of American Architecture.* New York: Harper & Row, 1979.

Sanderson, Arlene, ed. *Wright Sites.* River Forest: The Frank Lloyd Wright Building Conservancy, 1991.

Sargeant, J. *Frank Lloyd Wright Usonian Homes.* New York: Braziller, 1978.

Secrest, Meryle. *Frank Lloyd Wright: A Biography.* New York: Harper-Perennial, 1993.

Tafel, Edgar. *Years with Frank Lloyd Wright: Apprentice to Genius.* New York: Dover Publications, Inc., 1979.

Towmbly, Robert. *Frank Lloyd Wright: His Life and His Architecture.* New York: John Wiley, 1979.

Wright, Olgivanna. *Frank Lloyd Wright: His Life His Work His Words.* New York: Horizon Press, 1966.

Index

125

127

Photo Acknowledgments

The photographs and illustrations have been reproduced by permission of: Frank Lloyd Wright drawings are copyright © 1996 The Frank Lloyd Wright Foundation, pp. 1, 2–3 (background), 8; Courtesy The Frank Lloyd Wright Archives, pp. 2, 12 (both), 14, 15, 22, 27, 39, 43, 44, 52 (both), 54, 59, 67, 71, 74, 78, 82, 84, 86, 93, 96, 97, 98, 100, 101, 102, 105, 111 (both), 112, 114, 115, 116, 117; Photograph by Samuel Stewart, courtesy of the Western Pennsylvania Conservancy, p. 6; Courtesy of the Western Pennsylvania Conservancy, pp. 10, 11; The Frank Lloyd Wright Home and Studio Foundation: p. 16 [negative #H1090], p. 32 [negative #H133B], p. 33 [negative #H92], p. 36 [negative #H122], p. 37 [negative #H121], p. 46 [negative #H273], p. 48 [negative #H100], p. 50 [negative #H132], p. 62 [negative #H207], p. 85 [negative #H1071], p. 90 [negative #H1066]; State Historical Society of Wisconsin: p. 20 [negative #WHi(D3)7], p. 56 [negative #WHi(Howe)temp.18], p. 57 (top) [negative #WHi(X3)21674], p. 57 (bottom) [negative #WHi(Howe)temp.17], p. 64 [negative #WHi(X3)21080], p. 109 [negative #WHi(X3)26619], p. 118 [negative #WHiLot 3365/58A/18]; Frank Lloyd Wright drawings are copyright © 1995 The Frank Lloyd Wright Foundation, pp. 34, 42, 58, 68, 83, 88, 95, 120; Chicago Historical Society, photo #HB-04414-W, by Hedrich-Blessing, p. 91; Iowa DNR photo, Ken Formanek, p. 110.

Front cover portrait courtesy of The Frank Lloyd Wright Archives. Front cover photography courtesy of the Western Pennsylvania Conservancy. Back cover illustration: Frank Lloyd Wright drawings are copyright © 1995 The Frank Lloyd Wright Foundation.